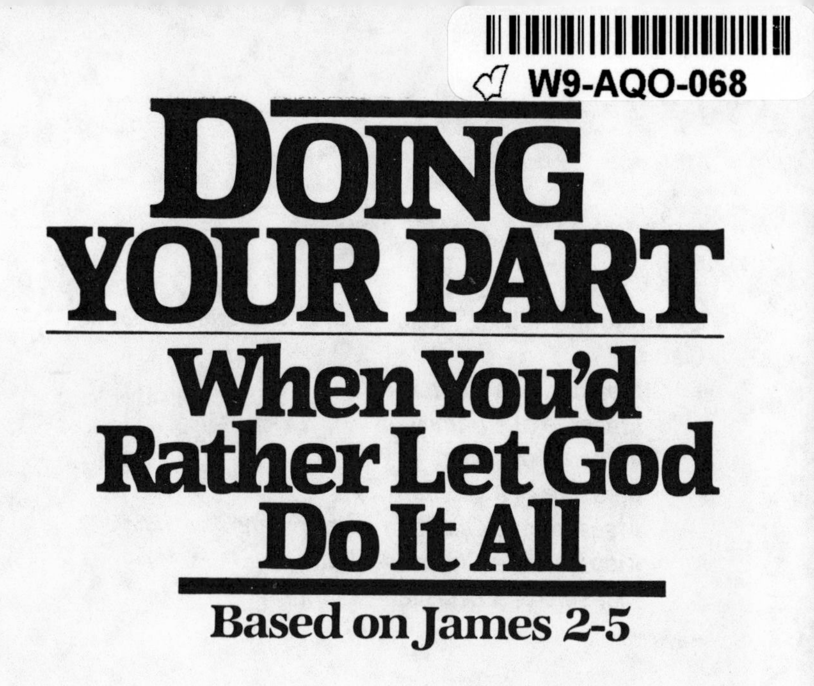

Doing Your Part When You'd Rather Let God Do It All

Based on James 2-5

Gene A. Getz

Regal Books
A Division of GL Publications
Ventura, California, U.S.A.

Other books in the "Measure of . . ." series by Gene A. Getz:

Measure of a Church
Measure of a Family
Measure of a Man
Measure of a Woman
Measure of a Christian—Philippians
Measure of a Christian—Titus
Measure of a Christian—James 1

The translation of all Regal books is under the direction of GLINT. GLINT provides technical help for the adaptation, translation and publishing of books for millions of people worldwide. For information regarding translation contact: GLINT, P.O. Box 6688, Ventura, California 93006.

Published by Regal Books
A Division of GL Publications
Ventura, California 93006
Printed in U.S.A.

Library of Congress Cataloging in Publication Data

Getz, Gene A.
Doing your part when you'd rather let God do it all.

Includes bibliographical references.
1. Bible. N.T. James II–V—Commentaries.
I. Bible. N.T. James II–V. English. New International. 1984. II. Title.
BS2785.3.G47 1984 227'.91077 84-17749
ISBN 0-8307-1002-7

CONTENTS

WHY THIS STUDY? 5
1. THE PERIL OF PREJUDICE 7
James 2:1-13
2. FAITH THAT FUNCTIONS 19
James 2:14-26
3. TAMING THE TONGUE 35
James 3:1-12
4. HEAVENLY WISDOM vs. EARTHLY WISDOM 51
James 3:13-18
5. FRIEND OF THE WORLD! ENEMY OF GOD! 66
James 4:1-6a
6. THE PERIL OF PRIDE 82
James 4:6b-10
7. THE SIN OF SLANDER 96
James 4:11-12
8. THE UNCERTAINTY OF LIFE 109
James 4:13-17
9. THE WAGES OF WORLDLY WEALTH 123
James 5:1-6
10. PATIENCE AND PERSEVERANCE IN PAIN 138
James 5:7-12
11. PROVISIONS THROUGH PRAYER 152
James 5:13-15
12. SICKNESS AND SIN 167
James 5:16-20

WHY THIS STUDY?

Of all New Testament books, the epistle of James focuses on "developing the mind of Christ." Furthermore, it is intensely personal. Though much of what is written is directed to "believers in relationship," great portions of the letter are directed to individual Christians and what should characterize their personal life style.

If you'll let Him, the Holy Spirit will use this study to "renew your mind," enabling you to "test and prove what God's will is." And as you do, you'll be able to contribute significantly to helping your fellow Christians—*as a body* of believers—also develop the mind of Christ. In that sense, Paul's prayer for the Romans will be answered in your own church—"that with *one heart* and *mind* you may glorify the God and Father of our Lord Jesus Christ" (Rom. 15:5).

RENEWAL—A BIBLICAL PERSPECTIVE

Renewal is the essence of dynamic Christianity and the basis on which Christians, both in a corporate or "body" sense and as individual believers, can determine the will of God. Paul made this clear when he wrote to the Roman Christians—"be transformed by the *renewing of your mind*. Then" he continued "you will be able to test and prove what God's will is" (Rom. 12:2). Here Paul is talking about renewal in a corporate sense. In other words, Paul is asking these Christians as a *body* of believers, to develop the mind of Christ through corporate renewal.

Personal renewal will not happen as God intended it unless it happens in the context of corporate renewal. On the other hand, corporate renewal will not happen as God intended without personal renewal. Both are necessary.

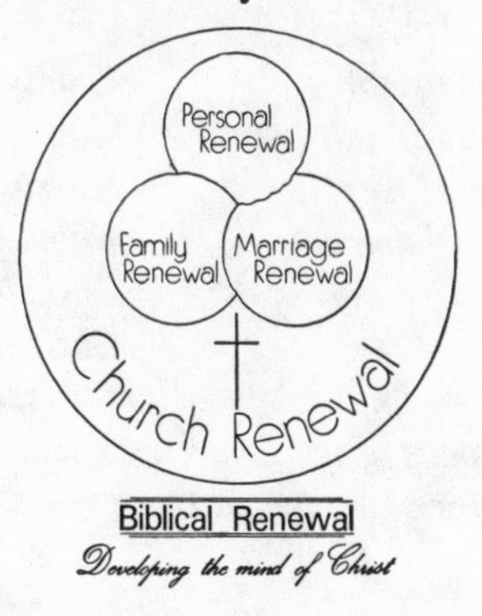

The larger circle represents "church renewal." This is the most comprehensive concept in the New Testament. However, every local church is made up of smaller self-contained, but interrelated units. The *family* in Scripture emerges as the "church in miniature." In turn, the family is made up of an even smaller social unit—*marriage*. The third inner circle represents *personal* renewal, which is inseparably linked to all of the other basic units. Marriage is made up of two separate individuals who become one. The family is made up of parents and children who are also to reflect the mind of Christ. And the church is made up of not only individual Christians, but couples and families.

Though all of these social units are interrelated, biblical renewal can begin within any specific social unit. But wherever it begins—in the church, families, marriages or individuals—the process immediately touches all the other social units. And one thing is certain! All that God says is consistent and harmonious. He does not have one set of principles for the church and another set for the family, another for husbands and wives and another for individual Christians. For example, the principles God outlines for local church elders, fathers and husbands regarding their role as leaders are interrelated and consistent. If they are not, we can be sure that we have not interpreted God's plan accurately.

The books listed below are part of the Biblical Renewal Series by Gene Getz designed to provide supportive help in moving toward renewal. They all fit into one of the circles described above and will provoke thought, provide interaction and tangible steps toward growth.

ONE ANOTHER SERIES

Building Up One Another

Encouraging One Another

Loving One Another

PERSONALITY SERIES

Abraham
David
Joseph
Joshua
Moses
Nehemiah

THE MEASURE OF SERIES

Measure of a . . .
Church
Family
Man
Marriage
Woman
Christian—Philippians
Christian—Titus
Christian—James 1

Sharpening the Focus of the Church presents an overall perspective for Church Renewal. All of these books are available from your bookstore.

1

THE PERIL OF PREJUDICE

James 2:1-13

My brothers, as believers in our glorious Lord Jesus Christ, don't show favoritism. Suppose a man comes into your meeting wearing a gold ring and fine clothes, and a poor man in shabby clothes also comes in. If you show special attention to the man wearing fine clothes and say, "Here's a good seat for you," but say to the poor man, "You stand there," or "Sit on the floor by my feet," have you not discriminated among yourselves and become judges with evil thoughts?

Listen, my dear brothers: Has not God chosen those who are poor in the eyes of the world to be rich in faith and to inherit the kingdom he promised those who love him? But you have insulted the poor. Is it not the rich who are exploiting you? Are they not the ones who are dragging you into court? Are they not the ones who are slandering the noble name of him to whom you belong?

If you really keep the royal law found in Scripture, "Love your neighbor as yourself," you are doing right. But if you show favoritism, you sin and are convicted by the law as lawbreakers. For who-

ever keeps the whole law and yet stumbles at just one point is guilty of breaking all of it. For he who said, "Do not commit adultery," also said, "Do not murder." If you do not commit adultery but do commit murder, you have become a lawbreaker.

Speak and act as those who are going to be judged by the law that gives freedom, because judgment without mercy will be shown to anyone who has not been merciful. Mercy triumphs over judgment! (James 2:1-13)

Two ministers, given to arguing about their respective faiths, were in a heated discussion. "That's all right," said one calmly. "We'll just agree to disagree. After all, we're both doing the Lord's work—you in your way and I in *His.*"

All of us, to some degree or another, face the problem of prejudice. It is a social disease that affects all ages. James, in chapter 2, deals with the manifestation of prejudice—*showing favoritism or partiality.* What he wrote represents one of the most specific scriptural indictments of Christians who fall prey to this kind of behavior.

JAMES'S BASIC EXHORTATION (James 2:1)

James came right to the point. He began by stating his concern succinctly. "My brothers, *as believers in our glorious Lord Jesus Christ,* don't show favoritism" (Jas. 2:1).

Inherent in this exhortation is a striking contrast—the behavior of some of these New Testament Christians and that of the Lord Jesus Christ! The Saviour, more than any other man who walked the face of this earth, was free of prejudice and of showing favoritism. It is true, He came unto His own people, the Jews. But this was merely a means to a divine end—to provide salvation for *all people.*

Peter, one of the twelve apostles, had to learn this lesson. As a Jew, he was exceptionally prejudiced against Gentiles, even after his conversion to Jesus Christ, and even after God had used him dramatically as a primary figure in launching the church. Consequently, the Lord had to communicate with Peter in an unusual way to help him overcome his prejudice.

On one occasion, about noontime, Peter ascended a stairway to the roof of a house in the city of Joppa to spend some time in prayer. While there he became hungry. But while he was waiting for a meal to be prepared, he "fell into a trance" (Acts 10:10). While in this state he had a vision. He saw a sheet being let down from heaven filled with all kinds of animals, including some that were "unclean" according to Jewish law. The voice of the Lord told him to "kill and eat." But Peter resisted, informing the Lord that he had *never* eaten anything unclean. Two more times the Lord commanded Peter to "kill and eat." And two more times Peter resisted.

And then something almost as dramatic happened! *Three* men, all Gentiles, appeared at the front door requesting that Peter come down to Caesarea at the invitation of another Gentile named Cornelius. Cornelius was a well-known centurion, and although a Gentile, "he and all his family were devout and God-fearing;" in fact, we read that "he gave generously to those in need and prayed to God regularly" (Acts 10:2). He, too, had received a vision in which an angel told him to invite Peter to his house.

Peter responded, and while he was there the Holy Spirit fell on Cornelius and his whole household and they were all converted to Jesus Christ. Amazed, and no doubt somewhat perplexed, Peter uttered a revealing statement: "I *now* realize how true it is that *God does not show favoritism* but accepts men from every nation who fear him and do what is right." Continuing, he shared an insight that previously had eluded him. "This is the message God sent to the people of Israel, telling the good news of peace through Jesus Christ, who is *Lord of all*" (Acts 10:34-36).

This was the very same message James was communicating in his letter. It is contradictory to claim to be a *believer* in the "glorious Lord Jesus Christ" and yet to show favoritism. To be His disciple means to live as He lived and to obey His commandments.

An Illustration (James 2:2-4)

Following his basic exhortation, James gave a specific illustration to get his point across, an illustration that focused on a particular problem in the New Testament world. Some of these Christians were showing favoritism to rich people by providing them with special considerations, while at the same time they were withholding certain considerations from poor people. "Suppose," James wrote, "a man comes into your meeting wearing a gold ring and fine clothes, and a poor man in shabby clothes also comes in. If you show special attention to the man wearing fine clothes and say, 'Here's a good seat for you,' but say to the poor man, 'You stand there,' or 'Sit on the floor by my feet,' have you not discriminated among yourselves and become judges with evil thoughts?" (Jas. 2:2-4).

At this juncture it is important to point out what James was *not* saying. He was *not* saying it is wrong to give honor to those to whom honor is due. He was *not* saying it is inappropriate to acknowledge with gratitude certain Christians who do special things for the Body of Christ. And certainly this involves material help.

The apostles illustrate this point with Barnabas. They even changed his name because of his generosity relative to his material possessions (see Acts 4:36-37). To change a person's name to conform to his life-style and to record it in Scripture is about as "public" as you can get in honoring a Christian for his unusual contributions.

What then was James saying? While *honoring* some, these New Testament Christians were *dishonoring* others. They were allocating them to a "lower position" because they were poor. This, implies James, is terribly wrong and sinful. It is discriminating and out of harmony with Christian theology.

An Explanation (James 2:5-7)

James went on to elaborate. "Listen, my dear brothers," he wrote. "Has not God chosen those who are poor in the eyes of the world to be rich in faith and to inherit the kingdom he promised those who love him?" (Jas. 2:5).

In other words, James was teaching that God does not discriminate. Some of those who had the least in the "kingdom of this world" had the most in the "kingdom of God." They may have been poor in material possessions, but they were rich in faith. Therefore, they should be treated equally as heirs and joint-heirs with Jesus Christ.

James went on to point out that some of these New Testament Christians—perhaps the leaders in the church—had "insulted the poor" and at the same time honored those who had exploited and mistreated them. They were even giving special honor to people who brought reproach on the name of Jesus Christ. This indeed would be an insult! This is the height of prejudice and favoritism—to relegate wealthy unbelievers who are hostile toward Christ to a position of prominence in the Christian community while assigning poor believers to a place of less prominence.

Our Motivation (James 2:8-11)

James next moved from his specific illustration and explanation to more general teaching on the subject of showing favoritism. He made reference to the "royal law" found in Scripture—both in the Old Testament and now in the New Testament. That law is to "love your neighbor as yourself."

When one of the teachers of the law came to Jesus and asked Him which was the most important of all the commandments, Jesus responded by linking two commandments together. "The most important one," answered Jesus, "is this: 'Hear, O Israel, the Lord our God, the Lord is one. Love the Lord your God with all your heart and with all your soul and with all your mind and with all your strength.'" At this point Jesus was quoting Moses (Deut. 6:4-5). However, Jesus went on to say, "The second is this: 'Love your neighbor as yourself.' There is no commandment greater than these" (Mark 12:29-31). And Matthew, in his gospel gives us an additional insight from Jesus relative to these statements. "All the Law and the Prophets hang on these two commandments," Jesus said (Matt. 22:40).

With this first statement, Jesus was summarizing the first four of the Ten Commandments—those that have to do with our relationship with God. Jesus' second statement summarized the final six commandments—those that have to do with our relationships with one another.

James then is zeroing in on our relationships with one another as Christians. We are to "accept one another" just as Christ has accepted us (Rom. 15:7).

To show favoritism is a violation of this royal law (Jas. 2:9). It is sin. But, when we love one another as Christ taught, we are being obedient to the royal law. Our relationships will be proper in all aspects of life.

Paul's teaching in Romans 13 makes this point even clearer. He wrote: "Let no debt remain outstanding, except the continuing debt to love one another, for he who loves his fellow man has fulfilled the law. The commandments, 'Do not commit adultery,' 'Do not murder,' 'Do not steal,' 'Do not covet,' and whatever other commandment there may be, are summed up in this one rule: *'Love your neighbor as yourself.'* Love does no harm to its neighbor. Therefore love is the fulfillment of the law" (Rom. 13:8-10).

The love of Jesus Christ breaks down all barriers—racial, ethnic, economic, and religious.

John Wesley once dreamed that he was at the gates of hell. He knocked and asked, "Are there any Roman Catholics here?" "Yes, many," was the reply. "Any Church of England men?" "Yes, many." "Any Presbyterians?" "Yes, many." "Any Wesleyans here?" "Yes, many."

Disappointed and dismayed, especially at the last reply, in his dream he turned his steps upward and found himself at the gates of paradise. Here he repeated the same questions. Finally he asked, "Any Wesleyans here?" "No," came the response. "Whom then have you here?" he asked in astonishment. "We do not know of any here which you have named. The only name of which we know anything here is 'Christian.'"

Paul wrote to the Ephesians, "There is one body and one Spirit—just as you were called to one hope when you were called—*one* Lord, *one* faith, *one* baptism, *one* God *and* Father of *all,* who is over *all* and through *all* and in *all*" (Eph. 4:4-6). That is the way it will be in heaven and that is the way it *should be* on earth.

A FINAL EXHORTATION (James 2:12-13)

James concludes this section of the sin of partiality and favoritism with a final exhortation. "Speak and act," he wrote, "as those who are going to be judged by the law that gives freedom, because judgment without mercy will be shown to anyone who has not been merciful. Mercy triumphs over judgment!" (Jas. 2:12-13).

The "law that gives freedom" is the "law of love," especially as that love was revealed in Jesus Christ. Thus Jesus said to His disciples shortly before He went to the cross—"A new commandment I give you: Love one another. As I have loved you, so you must love one another" (John 13:34).

It is this law that sets us free—free from prejudice and partiality. If we truly understand the love of Christ for us, there is no way we can continue to practice favoritism. If we "accept one another . . . just as Christ accepted" us, we cannot continue to reflect partiality in our relationships with others.

Think for a moment of what Paul was saying! When we come to Jesus Christ for salvation, He did not say I will accept you *if* you are from a certain economic background. He did not say I will accept you *if* you wear certain kinds of clothes; *if* you have a gold ring on your finger; *if* you are a certain color; *if* you come from a certain ethnic background; *if* you are Baptist or Catholic. Rather, Jesus accepts us just as we are—rich or poor, German or Swede, black or white, Jew or Gentile, Baptist or Catholic. And that is the way Christians are to accept one another. There are to be no conditions attached to our relationships.

In Christ we are set free to practice this kind of love. Unfortunately, not all Christians do. If they did, James would not have had to write so specifically about showing favoritism. This was a first-century problem which often appears in the twentieth century.

A TWENTIETH-CENTURY ILLUSTRATION

I was deeply moved by a story told by Bernie May, who serves with Wycliffe Bible Translators and was formerly executive director of Wycliffe's Jungle Aviation and Radio Services (JAARS). He has been a missionary pilot for over twenty-five years. On one occasion a large church invited him to be a special guest so they could present an airplane as a gift to JAARS. "It was a Bible-believing church," Bernie relates, "filled with scrubbed-faced fundamentalists—the kind I like to be around. I was the main speaker for the Sunday morning service—a real VIP."

His story continues. "During Sunday School a friend introduced me to a beautiful black woman, who was visiting the church for the first time, because she learned I was to speak. I immediately recognized her, although we had never met. She was Josephine Makil, a Wycliffe translator home on furlough from Viet Nam.

"Some months before, she and her family had been ambushed on a lonely Viet Nam road. She and three of her children had watched in horror as her husband and the fourth child he was holding in his arms were murdered in cold blood. She is one of God's special people.

"That morning, before I spoke, I introduced Josephine asking her and the children to stand. She gave a brief but powerful testimony, closing by saying, 'I can testify that God's ways are perfect and His grace is sufficient.'

"The words burned deep in my heart," Bernie stated. "I wanted to remove my shoes, so hallowed was the ground as I stood beside her. It took me long moments before I could speak. I couldn't get the lump out of my throat.

"After the service the people flocked around me shaking my hand and patting my back. During the adulation I happened to look to one side. There stood Josephine and the children. Alone. In fact, the people were deliberately avoiding her. She was black.

"I could hardly restrain my anger," Bernie states. "I wanted to rush through that magnificent building, overturning the pews and shouting, 'Keep your money. Keep your handshakes. Keep your airplane. It goes up as a stench before God.'

"But," said Bernie, "I didn't. Perhaps I was too much the coward. I did break from the group and go to Josephine. We chatted, but she said nothing about her rejection. She reacted to those church people the same way she reacted to those who murdered her husband—with love and forgiveness.

"These people found it strange that God could use a black person like Josephine. I, in turn, found it strange that God would use people like those in that church; yet their gift has been a blessing to the kingdom.

"But then, I'm sure some folks find it strange that God would use a fellow like me.

"Josephine is right. Love is the only way to react. For all our sakes, we must leave judgment to God."[1]

Bernie May *is* right. We must leave judgment to God. But God says that He will bring judgment "without mercy" on those who have not "been merciful"; even on Christians!

Don't misunderstand! Christians will not stand before the Great White Throne Judgment Seat to be judged for their sins. Only those who do not know Jesus Christ personally will be there. However, every Christian will stand before the Judgment Seat of Christ. It is there we will be rewarded according to the way in which we have been obedient to God's Word. The Judgment Seat of Christ involves rewards. And Paul says that our "work will be shown for what it is, because the Day will bring it to light. It will be revealed with fire, and the fire will test the quality of each man's work" (1 Cor. 3:13).

A PERSONAL CONFESSION

To what extent am I free from prejudice and from showing favoritism and partiality? Even more specifically, to what extent am I free from judging others and forming opinions that are based on improper motives and/or ignorance? And even more important, to what extent do I verbalize (use my tongue) and visualize (use body language) to demonstrate those attitudes of prejudice and cause feelings of rejection and hurt in other people?

As I reflect on my own background, I can see how prejudiced I had become because of what I was taught in childhood. I had grown up in a restrictive and legalistic religious community. It was an ethnic community as well. For years I was taught overtly and covertly that I was better than other people because of my religious and cultural heritage. All other people who called themselves "Christians" were wrong. *I* had the truth. No one else did.

Though I rejected those attitudes after I became a true Christian, I did not realize, at first, how much they had become a part of the fabric of my personality. Those prejudiced feelings lingered in my heart. I can see now that God used some very painful and disillusioning experiences in my life to help me break out of my narrow, provincial, and subtle prejudice. It was only as I was "reaching up to touch bottom" that I realized how much I needed other people who were not from my own religious and social background.

Prejudice and pride must be dealt with if we're going to follow Jesus Christ. We all struggle with these problems. It is only by God's grace that we are what we are. We must realize that "God is no respecter of persons." His grace and love are for all.

AREAS OF PREJUDICE

Following are some areas where we can all get trapped and find ourselves revealing prejudices and partiality. Check yourself.

My Attitudes and Actions Towards:

☐ those who do not have as much as I do materially

☐ those who have more than I do materially

☐ those who do not have as much education as I do

☐ those who have more education than I do

☐ those who have a more prestigious position than I do

☐ those who have a less prestigious position than I do

☐ those who have more talent and fewer skills than I do

☐ those who have less talent and skill than I do

☐ those older than I am

☐ those younger than I am

☐ those who come from a different ethnic background than I do

☐ those who come from a different religious background than I do

☐ if married, my attitudes and actions towards singles

☐ if single, my attitudes and actions towards marrieds

☐ Other: ______________________________

____

Note

1. Bernie May, *Under His Wing* (Portland, OR: Multnomah Press, 1979), pp. 41-42.

2

FAITH THAT FUNCTIONS
James 2:14-26

"What good is it, my brothers, if a man claims to have faith but has no deeds? Can such faith save him? Suppose a brother or sister is without clothes and daily food. If one of you says to him, "Go, I wish you well; keep warm and well fed," but does nothing about his physical needs, what good is it? In the same way, faith by itself, if it is not accompanied by action, is dead.

But someone will say, "You have faith; I have deeds."

Show me your faith without deeds, and I will show you my faith by what I do. You believe that there is one God. Good! Even the demons believe that—and shudder.

You foolish man, do you want evidence that faith without deeds is useless? Was not our ancestor Abraham considered righteous for what he did when he offered his son Isaac on the altar? You see that his faith and his actions were working together, and his faith was made complete by what he did. And the

> *scripture was fulfilled that says, "Abraham believed God, and it was credited to him as righteousness," and he was called God's friend. You see that a person is justified by what he does and not by faith alone.*
>
> *In the same way, was not even Rahab the prostitute considered righteous for what she did when she gave lodging to the spies and sent them off in a different direction? As the body without the spirit is dead, so faith without deeds is dead.* (James 2:14-26)

The Epistle of James has been attacked more than any other book in the Bible. Even Martin Luther called this little letter "an epistle of straw." This may surprise you. However, once we understand Luther's background, we can understand why he reacted to what James wrote.

For years, Luther tried to become righteous before God by living an austere and regimented life as a monk. He performed his tasks faithfully, went to confession regularly, and religiously carried out the penances imposed on him for his sins.

However, Luther never found peace with God by "performing" all of these works. But, through careful study of the Scriptures, eventually the marvelous truth that salvation is a free gift obtained only by faith flooded his weary soul. Paul's letters to the Romans and Galatians became a special means in unlocking this truth in Luther's heart. "But now a righteousness from God, apart from law, has been made known, to which the Law and the Prophets testify," wrote Paul. *"This righteousness from God comes through faith in Jesus Christ to all who believe"* (Rom. 3:21-22). And to the Galatians, Paul wrote: "The righteous will live by faith" (Gal. 3:11). It was this great theological truth that set Martin Luther free from his emotional and spiritual bondage. This experience impacted his own life and eventually the whole religious and secular world as well. Luther became a prime mover in causing a Protestant Reformation. He became a champion for *sola fide* (faith alone) and *sola gratia* (grace alone). Furthermore, he proclaimed through both his lectures and writings the great truth, *sola scriptura* (the Bible alone) for faith and practice.

When studying the Epistle of James, particularly the passage we're looking at in this chapter, Luther concluded that James was contradicting Paul. It is easy to see why. First, he had been reared in a religious community where he had been taught that a person gets to heaven by performing good works. Through personal study of the Scriptures he discovered that this was a false doctrine. Consequently, he literally put his life on the line for the doctrine of justification by faith. From his cultural perspective we can see why he might misunderstand and overreact to what James was saying and teaching.

What *was* James teaching? Let's look carefully at this passage.

TRUE FAITH EXEMPLIFIED (James 2:14-17)

This section of James's letter is a central focus for his whole Epistle. What he wrote in verses 14 to 26 summarizes his major concern. Everything he wrote before and after this passage illustrates and elaborates upon this concern. James believed that *true* faith functions! It is exemplified with good works!

To get this point across, James begins with two questions—

- "What good is it, my brothers, if a man claims to have faith but has no deeds?" (Jas. 2:14a).
- "Can such faith save him?" (2:14b).

To make his point James used the same technique he

used earlier in this chapter to illustrate the sin of showing favoritism (compare 2:2). He posed a hypothetical situation, no doubt based on reality. "Suppose," James wrote, "a brother or sister is without clothes and daily food. If one of you says to him, 'Go, I wish you well; keep warm and well fed,' but does nothing about his physical needs, what good is it? In the same way," James concluded, *"faith by itself, if it is not accompanied by action, is dead"* (2:15-17).

"Dead Faith"—What Is It? (James 2:17,26)

Twice in this passage James referred to "dead faith" (Jas. 2:17,26). What did he mean?

Note first that James wrote, "If a man *claims* to have faith," not "If a man *has* faith." These two statements are quite different in meaning. The whole of Scripture teaches that it is possible to claim faith in God and Jesus Christ and yet not be saved. James made this clear in verse 19 when he said, "You believe there is one God. Good! Even the demons believe that—and shudder" (2:19).

Throughout his gospel, John made many references to "believing," but in many instances those who *claimed* to believe in Jesus Christ did not demonstrate that their faith was *saving* faith. For example, on one occasion after Jesus had fed thousands of people by multiplying the loaves and fishes, He went on to teach the true meaning of being His follower. "I tell you the truth," Jesus explained, "unless you eat the flesh of the Son of Man and drink his blood, you have no life in you. Whoever eats my flesh and drinks my blood has eternal life, and I will raise him up at the last day" (John 6:53-54). Here Jesus was talking about what it *really* means to believe and become His follower. He did not mean that we are to partake literally of His flesh and blood. Rather, Christ was referring to that act of faith whereby we actually receive Him into our lives, making Him a very part of our inner being. Just as food and drink become a part of our physical being, so Jesus Christ should become a part of our spiritual being.

On this occasion many of those who *claimed* to believe in Jesus and identified with Him as His disciples, simply responded: "This is a hard teaching. Who can accept it?" (John 6:60). And then we read, "From this time *many of His disciples* turned back and no longer followed him" (6:66). Their faith was not "living faith"—it was "dead." Rather than asking for further explanation, they walked away from the One who had met their physical needs so bountifully the day before when He multiplied the loaves and fishes.

This is why John concluded his gospel with this statement: "These [miracles] are written that you may believe that Jesus is the Christ, the Son of God, and that by *believing* you may have life in his name" (John 20:31). There is faith that produces eternal life. There is faith that does not. When it does *not* produce eternal life, James says that it is "dead" faith (Jas. 2:17). Eternal life is missing.

To make this point clear, James used another illustration in verse 26. He referred to a corpse—a dead person. Though rather graphic, it does illustrate what "dead faith" actually is. "As a body without the spirit is dead, so faith without deeds is dead" (Jas. 2:26). In other words, just as there is no "life" in a "dead body," so there is no "eternal life" in a "dead faith."

TRUE FAITH VERIFIED (James 2:18)

How Can We Discern if "Faith" Is "True Faith"?

There are some questions regarding the actual translation and meaning of James 2:18. However, from the overall context, it seems that James used a dramatic technique to make his next point. As if being present with them, he turned to one person in the congregation, and said, "You have faith"; that is, "You *claim* to have faith." He then turned to another person who had said, "I have deeds." He then seemingly turned to the congregation as a whole and gave a personal testimony: "Show me your faith without deeds, and I will show you my faith by what I do" (2:18). The test of true faith, wrote James, is what it produces in our lives as Christians. If there is no *fruit,* there is no *root.* It is dead faith. If it is true faith, there will eventually be deeds and actions.

"Deeds" and "Actions"—What Are They?

A specific illustration. In the previous paragraph James had already fleshed out the evidence of "true faith" with an illustration of "dead faith." He set up a hypothetical situation which, as with favoritism, was probably based on reality. He referred to the brother or sister "without clothes and daily food" (Jas. 2:15).

Note first that James was speaking of having a *true* need. He referred to a poor person who did not have the necessities of life. There's nothing more basic than clothes and food. Without clothes we might survive for a time, depending on the weather conditions. Without food, we'll eventually die, no matter what the weather conditions.

At this point let me insert a word of caution. In our present society there are "professional beggars" who go from church to church taking advantage of believers. As a pastor I have encountered them rather frequently. They have well-organized stories about their personal misfortunes and tragedies. For example, a girl called our church asking for financial help to pay her rent. She said she was divorced, had several children, didn't have enough money to pay her rent, and was about to be evicted from her apartment and put out in the street. We did not want to turn our back on a person in need. But we've learned to ask questions to determine if a particular request is valid.

In order to verify her story, we asked for the phone number of the apartment manager. "Yes," he reported. "I am going to have to evict her if she doesn't come up with the money."

We then called her again and asked her and her children to meet us at our Friday night church service. At this point she began to resist and became evasive. Eventually, she responded negatively and the conversation was terminated. Then we began to see the true picture. No doubt, even the "apartment manager" was a setup—perhaps her boyfriend. It was all a scheme to get money. Together they were probably going from church to church, and doing quite well.

James, of course, is talking about a *true* need—a brother or sister without sufficient clothes and food and no way to get help. Work opportunities are nonexistent, and there is no other source of income.

In James's illustration this poor person was turned away by those who claimed to be Christians. Though these people wished him well, they did "nothing about his physical needs" (2:16). This, said James, reflects "dead faith." There is no action, no works, no evidence of what true faith produces.

Though illustrated negatively, the positive point is clear. Christians who do care, who do respond to people's true needs are demonstrating James's later statement: "I will show you my faith by what I do."

In our church we have small groups called "Fellowship Families" and "mini-churches." They are led by lay pastors. Periodically, in the group there are people who go through crises where they find it impossible to care for their own needs. I have observed situations where a group of Christians at such times rally around these people in need and literally put food on their table until they can "dig themselves out" of the crisis. Were he here, I believe

James would have been pleased with these acts of love.

There are times, of course, when we have to deal with people who take advantage of these opportunities for help. But seldom does this happen with people who are committed to the group as regular attenders.

A larger perspective. The total context of James leaves no room for questions regarding what he meant by faith that functions. This can be illustrated by the comparisons on the facing pages:

Note that each column represents a profile. Furthermore, it is possible for a person to have *true faith* and yet appear to others as if his faith is *dead.* The Corinthians illustrated this point dramatically. In fact, Paul stated clearly that if it were not for God's unusual gifts to these people at the moment of conversion, there would be no evidence they were true believers. And yet, Paul recognized that they were, even though their lives reflected carnality and worldliness (1 Cor. 1:4-9; 3:1-3).

Because the Corinthians' faith was real, eventually their lives began to change. They responded to Paul's exhortations and began to follow the leadership of the Holy Spirit. The life within began to come to the surface and became visible to others. So it will, agreed James!

TRUE FAITH PERSONIFIED (James 2:20-26)

Under certain circumstances, true faith is always verified by deeds and actions. James then went on to illustrate this point with two Old Testament personalities.

It is at this point that some Christians get confused. In fact, it is at this very point that Martin Luther concluded that James was not teaching the same doctrine as the Apostle Paul. And if James was teaching salvation by works, as Luther himself once believed, he knew by experience that it was impossible to have peace with God by

Dead Faith	*References*	*True Faith*
Turns its back on needy people	(1:27; 2:15-16)	Helps people in need
Shows favoritism	(2:1-4)	Accepts others as equals in Christ
Causes people to curse others	(3:1-12; 4:11-12)	Causes people to praise God and bless others
Reflects earthly wisdom	(3:13-18)	Reflects heavenly wisdom
Causes fights and quarrels	(4:1-3)	Causes acceptance and unity
Results in worldliness	(4:4-6)	Leads to a holy and righteous life-style
Follows Satan's will	(4:7-10)	Submits to God's will
Leads to boasting and bragging	(4:13-17)	Leads to humility before God and men
Reflects materialism	(5:1-6)	Reflects spirituality
Wavers and "falls away" in the midst of suffering	(5:7-11)	Reflects patience in the midst of suffering
Focuses on self-effort	(5:13-18)	Focuses on prayer

trying to make yourself acceptable to God in your own strength.

Let's note what James wrote. "You foolish man, do you want evidence that faith without deeds is useless?" He then referred to two Old Testament personalities.

Abraham, the Patriarch (James 2:20-24)

James does make statements in this passage that sound diametrically opposed to Paul's teaching. *"Was not our ancestor, Abraham, considered righteous for what he did when he offered his son Isaac on the altar?"* James asked. "You see that his faith and his actions were working together, and his faith was made complete by what he did. And the scripture was fulfilled that says, 'Abraham believed God, and it was credited to him as righteousness,' and he was called God's friend. *You see that a person is justified by what he does and not by faith alone"* (Jas. 2:21-24).

There are at least two statements in this passage that sound contradictory to Paul's teaching. Note the comparison:

JAMES	*PAUL*
"Was not our ancestor Abraham considered righteous for what he did when he offered his son Isaac on the altar?" (Jas. 2:21).	"If, in fact, Abraham was justified by works, he had something to boast about—but not before God. What does the Scripture say, 'Abraham believed God, and it was credited to him as righteousness'" (Rom. 4:2-3).
"You see that a person is justified by what he does and not by faith alone" (Jas. 2:24).	"Therefore, since we have been justified through faith, we have peace with God through our Lord Jesus Christ" (Rom. 5:1).

What is a correct perspective on this passage? Why this apparent contradiction? What is James actually saying?

Let me say up front that I do not believe James was contradicting Paul. These men were in perfect harmony theologically. To understand this we need to view James's statement in the total context of Scripture.

There's a lot that could be said to clarify this passage of Scripture. Let me, however, make two brief observations.

First, if James were teaching salvation by faith plus works in this passage, he would be contradicting himself in the very same passage. In one breath he would be saying, "Abraham believed God, and it was credited to him as righteousness" (Jas. 2:23). And in the very next verse he would be denying that Abraham was justified by faith alone, for he wrote, "You see that a person is justified by what he does and not by faith alone" (2:24). It does not make sense, of course, that James—or any person in his right mind—would be guilty of such faulty thinking.

Second, both James and Paul recognized and acknowledged that Abraham's righteousness before God was based upon faith, and faith alone, when he first believed God thirty years before he was asked to offer Isaac.

Abraham's original experience, which both James and Paul referred to, is recorded in Genesis 15. The Lord had already promised that He would bless Abraham with children. To be specific, when the Lord first called Abraham to leave his homeland, He said, "I will make you into a great nation" (Gen. 12:2). Years later, after Abraham was settled in Canaan, God affirmed that promise. One evening the Lord called Abraham's attention to the multitude of stars in the heavens. "'Look up at the heavens and count the stars—if indeed you can count them.' Then he said to him, 'So shall your offspring be.'" And then we read a statement that both Paul and James quoted: *"Abram believed the LORD, and he credited it to him as righteous-*

ness" (Gen. 15:5-6; see also Rom. 4:3; Jas. 2:23).

The next experience referred to by James happened thirty years later and is recorded in Genesis 22. God tested Abraham in the very area where He had made His promise. He asked him to offer his son Isaac as a sacrifice. At this point, Abraham's faith in God's special promise was so strong that he truly believed that if God took his son in this way, He would bring him back to life (see Heb. 11:17-19). Thus, Abraham obeyed God, and just as he was ready to take his son's life on the altar the Lord intervened and said, "Now I know that you fear God, because you have not withheld from me your son, your only son" (Gen. 22:12).

What then was James saying? He was saying the same thing he had been saying all along in his Epistle—that true faith produces works. What Abraham did in response to God's request demonstrated both his faith and his righteousness. John Blanchard, generalizing on this truth, says, "James is not saying that faith plus works equals a Christian, but that true faith always produces works. This is the principle of faith. Faith is alive and active, and it works out from a believing heart into an obedient life."[1]

Rahab, the Prostitute (James 2:25-26)

James used one more illustration to make his point. He referred to Rahab, a prostitute, who lived in the city of Jericho. Before crossing over the Jordan, Joshua had sent two spies to check out the situation in Canaan. When they arrived in Jericho, they stayed in Rahab's house. However, the king of Jericho had his own secret service men at work. They followed Joshua's men to Rahab's home. And when orders came from the king to Rahab to expose these men of Israel, she hid them on her rooftop under some stocks of flax. Later, when the king's men left, Rahab acknowledged the one true God (see Josh. 2:11). In fact, there is evidence in this very chapter that Rahab had already changed her profession from prostitution to being a dyemaker and innkeeper. She had become a believer in the God of Abraham, Isaac, and Jacob *before* the spies even arrived at her home.[2]

How then was Rahab saved? She received salvation from the Lord in the same way every person has been saved since the dawn of history. It was by faith and faith alone.

Why then does James include her story in this passage? He's making the same point he made with Abraham's story: True faith produces works; it moves out from the heart and into the life. Rahab demonstrated that her faith in God was real with her willingness to give "lodging to the spies," knowing full well she would put her own life and the lives of her family in jeopardy. However, she trusted God in this situation, thus revealing the reality of her relationship with God.

A Summation

Chuck Swindoll clearly summarizes James's emphasis as compared with Paul's with the following chart:[3]

	PAUL'S MESSAGE	JAMES'S MESSAGE
Emphasis	Calls attention to the "root," looking at what happens *at* the moment of salvation	Calls attention to the "fruit," looking at what happens *after* salvation
Perspective	Focuses on *God's* part	Focuses on *man's* part
Terms	Deals with *justification*	Deals with *validation*

Spiros Zodhiates, in his excellent commentary on James, puts it all together with this statement:

> The summation of the whole chapter, then, the second of James, is, "Let us beware of hypocrisy." If we say we are Christians, let us live Christlike lives. If we believe, let us behave. If in us we have the Christ-given faith, from us let the Christlike behavior emanate.[4]

SOME PERSONAL REFLECTIONS

How should every individual respond to James's message in this passage?

First, if I claim to be saved, on what do I base my salvation?

Paul clarified this point very specifically in his letter in the Ephesians. He wrote: "For it is by grace you have been saved, through faith—and this not from yourselves, it is the gift of God—not by works, so that no one can boast" (Eph. 2:8-9).

Second, if I claim to have this kind of salvation experience, what evidence is there that my faith in Christ is real?

Again, Paul clarified the answer to this question in his letter to the Ephesians. After describing clearly how a person is saved, he said: "For we are God's workmanship, created in Christ Jesus *to do good works,* which God prepared in advance for us to do" (2:10).

NOTE:

1. It is possible to do good works and not to be saved. The world is filled with people who are trying to earn their way to heaven. The Bible teaches that this isn't possible.
2. It is possible to claim to believe in Jesus Christ and not be saved. This was the point that James was making.

3. It is possible to be truly saved and not living for Christ as we should. Again, this is a point that James is making. The world is filled with Christians who are infant Christians. Like the Corinthians, they have not grown in their spiritual lives.

In What Category Are You?

1. If you are in category one, attempting to earn your way to heaven, stop working and put your faith in Jesus Christ for salvation. Accept His free gift. This *must* be step number one.
2. If you are in category two and claim to be a Christian, but are not revealing your faith through deeds and good works, stop and ask yourself if you have truly put your faith in Jesus Christ. If you are not sure, be sure today. Rest assured, He will accept you. He will not turn you away.
3. Perhaps you are in category three. You *know* that your faith is real. But you also know that you are not living for Christ as you should. Would you then determine today to commit your life totally to Jesus Christ and let Him do His work through you? Consider Paul's words to the Philippians: "For it is God who works in you to will and to act according to his good purpose" (Phil. 2:13).

A FINAL THOUGHT

There is a story that the demons once held a conference. The purpose of the conference was to devise some effective method to do harm to the Lord's work on earth. One demon got up and said, "Let us go down and persuade men that there is no God." This, however, was rejected by the majority of the demons and by the archdemon, the devil, with the statement that it was impossible for any intelligent man not to believe in the existence of God. How could they persuade men of the nonexistence of God since they themselves believed that there is a God?

Then another demon got up and proposed that they should go down and tell the people that Jesus Christ never really existed and that men should not believe in fiction. This also was rejected, as the majority of the conferees said that historical facts are historical facts and that Jesus Christ is an historical figure that even demonic persuasion would not succeed in obliterating.

Then another demon got up and suggested that they should go down and persuade everyone that death ended it all and they should not worry about life after death. But this also was rejected because they said that man would come to the conclusion that God must have been a fool to have created man only for this earth.

And then, finally, the most intelligent of all the demons got up and said, "I'll tell you what we'll do. We'll go down and tell everybody to believe that there is a God, that there is Jesus Christ, that belief in Him saves, but you can get by by just professing faith and go on living in sin as you used to." Immediately this proposal was unanimously acclaimed, and ever since, the demons, Satan's agents, have been telling people to believe but not to behave as God wants them to.

Such belief is not saving faith, but represents "dead faith." It is of the devil. This is the message of James.

Notes

1. John Blanchard, *Not Hearers Only,* vol. 2 (London: Saventrust, 1981), p. 100.
2. Gene Getz, *Joshua* (Ventura, CA: Regal Books, 1979).
3. Charles R. Swindoll, *James,* Bible Study Guide, p. 39.
4. Spiros Zodhiates, *The Behavior of Belief* (Grand Rapids: Wm. B. Eerdmans Publishing Co., 1959), p. 72.

3

TAMING THE TONGUE
James 3:1-12

Not many of you should presume to be teachers, my brothers, because you know that we who teach will be judged more strictly. We all stumble in many ways. If anyone is never at fault in what he says, he is a perfect man, able to keep his whole body in check.

When we put bits into the mouths of horses to make them obey us, we can turn the whole animal. Or take ships as an example. Although they are so large and are driven by strong winds, they are steered by a very small rudder wherever the pilot wants to go. Likewise the tongue is a small part of the body, but it makes great boasts. Consider what a great forest is set on fire by a small spark. The tongue also is a fire, a world of evil among the parts of the body. It corrupts the whole person, sets the whole course of his life on fire, and is itself set on fire by hell.

All kinds of animals, birds, reptiles and creatures of the sea are being tamed and have been tamed by man, but no man can tame the tongue. It is a restless evil, full of deadly poison.

> *With the tongue we praise our Lord and Father, and with it we curse men, who have been made in God's likeness. Out of the same mouth come praise and cursing. My brothers, this should not be. Can both fresh water and salt water flow from the same spring? My brothers, can a fig tree bear olives, or a grapevine bear figs? Neither can a salt spring produce fresh water.* (James 3:1-12)

Someone has said:

> If your lips should keep from slips,
> Five things observe with care;
> Of whom you speak, to whom you speak,
> And how and when and where.

How true! Let me say it another way—

- When talking *about* others—be careful!
- When talking *to* others—be careful!
- When talking *about* others *to others,* be careful *how* you say it.
- When talking to others, about others, not only consider *how* you say it, but *when* you say it and *where* you say it.

This is good advice—in all situations and circumstances. However, James adds two more dimensions. He warns Christians to be careful about *what* they say and *why* they say it! In fact, this is more foundational than the people involved, the how, and the when and where.

A POSITIVE PERSPECTIVE (James 3:1-5a)

James opens this section of his letter with some positive thoughts about the tongue. As I stated in the first volume of *The Measure of a Christian, James 1,* our tongue can be our greatest asset or our greatest liability.[1] But first, James warns those in leadership positions.

A Word of Caution! (James 3:1)

"Not many of you should presume to be teachers, my brothers, because you know that we who teach will be judged more strictly" (Jas. 3:1).

There are several reasons James gave this warning. *First,* teachers in the church are in very responsible roles. The very position itself opens doors for influence and persuasion. In many respects we are in the "driver's" seat. People follow us and look to us for guidance. And how tragic to lead people in the wrong direction. Jesus said, "If a blind man leads a blind man, both will fall into a pit" (Matt. 15:14).

This warning, however, extends beyond the church. It involves the family. Children look to their parents for guidance. And in both the church and the home, it is often not so much *what* we say but *how* and *the way we live* out what we say that is of supreme importance. Someone has said that what we *do* speaks so loudly that others cannot *hear* what we say.

The *second* reason James gave this word of caution relates to what was actually happening in the New Testament world. The people he was writing to were Christians converted out of Judaism. As Jews these people were led by the rabbis, who were held in a very exalted position. The very name means "my great one." Consequently, these men often became proud and arrogant and "loved themselves" and "their positions" as an end in itself. They demonstrated their false motives by lording it over their followers and often heaping upon them burdens and requirements that were beyond their ability to bear. Ironically many of these leaders did not practice what they expected of others.

Jesus had some choice words for these men when He

said, "Everything they do is done for men to see: they make their phylacteries wide and the tassels of their prayer shawls long; they love the place of honor at banquets and the most important seats in the synagogues; they love to be greeted in the marketplaces and to have men call them 'Rabbi'" (Matt. 23:5-7).

Unfortunately, some of this carnal mentality crept into the Christian Church. Men particularly, many of whom were unqualified, sought "teaching positions." The tendency for this to happen was accentuated because of the very nature of the Church. The fact that every member of the Church was important in building up the Body of Christ opened the door for people to emerge and want to teach others. Unfortunately, many of them were not qualified to lead and speak openly to the Church and, furthermore, many of them had false motives. They were more interested in glorifying themselves than the Lord, and were not concerned with helping others grow in Christ.

Thus James gives a strong word of caution. What he had to say about the tongue has particular application to those who teach. With this kind of responsibility goes more accountability. "We who teach will be judged more strictly." The implication is clear. We should approach this kind of task with the spirit of humility and teachability. And one basic reflection of whether or not we are mature enough to be in a teaching role is *how* we use our tongue.

A Challenge to All (James 3:2)

James continued: "We *all* stumble in many ways. If anyone is never at fault in what he says, he is a perfect man, able to keep his whole body in check" (Jas. 3:2).

James first acknowledged that we all have weaknesses. We all fail God in various situations and circumstances. In a spirit of humility, he included himself. *"We,"* he wrote, "all stumble in many ways" (3:2a). None of us is exempt from making mistakes.

On the other hand, James wrote, "If anyone is never at fault in what he says, he is a perfect man, able to keep his whole body in check" (3:2b). On the surface this may sound contradictory to what he had just said. Not so! First, James was pointing out how important the tongue is in reflecting Christian maturity. It, out of every part of the body, reveals our inner being and what we really are. *If* we *never* make a mistake with our tongue we would indeed be perfect! But, James had already pointed out that this is impossible.

However, James set before these believers a goal—the challenge to become more and more like Christ. This, of course, had been his goal all along, and now he became specific as to how they might achieve that goal.

The word *perfect* can also be translated "mature"—to become an "adult" rather than to remain a "child" in our Christian experience. Though we will never be like Christ in every respect while on this earth, we can become more and more like Him and reach a level of maturity that indeed reflects the life of Jesus Christ—though always imperfectly.

Learning to control our tongue is in some respects like learning to ski—which is one of my favorite sports. Beginners always stumble and fall. There is no other way to learn. A mountain is no respecter of persons. Big people, little people, athletic types, nonathletic types—everybody learns to ski by learning to stand up. And in the process, everyone falls down.

But as you're learning, you discover how to control yourself. You learn to control the mountain rather than allowing the mountain to control you. You actually learn to use the mountain to your advantage.

As you progress, you also learn to ski more difficult slopes. First, you learn to master the beginner slopes.

Next, you move to the intermediate areas and finally to the advanced slopes. But with each step of progress, you tend to regress—often to a prone position—until you have mastered the next level of difficulty. In fact, I've often said that if you're not falling, you're not progressing.

Finally, you become an advanced skier. But, lo and behold, you find there is always more to learn. And even when you feel you're in total control, if you're not careful, you'll suddenly find yourself flat on your face or your back—depending on what happens at the moment.

I remember taking lessons from a ski instructor in Colorado. Beverly is one of the best! At the time I first got to know her she was a relatively new Christian. And each year I skied in this particular ski area, we worked out a deal. I'd be her spiritual instructor going up the ski lifts, if she'd be my ski instructor on the way down! It was a great arrangement. My advice was free and so was hers.

Most of what I've learned about skiing, I've learned from Beverly. The one thing I learned is that the best is not perfect. On one occasion, we were approaching the base of the mountain. She was out ahead of me demonstrating a particular maneuver. As she looked back to give me a word of wisdom, she suddenly caught an edge with her ski and went sprawling all over the mountain.

Inside I chuckled as I skied up beside her and asked her if she was okay. She was the best in my book—but she fell. However, in this instance I had enough sense not to laugh out loud. I knew then and there that no matter how good you are, you can make mistakes. Usually it happens when you're not concentrating; perhaps when you're tired; mostly when you're overconfident; and quite frequently when you're showing off. And you always fall when you're over your head, when you're trying new approaches, when you're stretching yourself. And it usually happens when you least expect it.

And so it is with the tongue. Learning to live successfully for Christ is a process. And we never arrive. We're never perfect. Mature? Yes! That is necessary to be in the will of God. But we're never exempt from failure along the way.

The Tongue Can Be Powerful for Good (James 3:2-5a)

James used two illustrations to demonstrate how powerful the tongue really is. He had already stated his proposition; that is, if a Christian can control his tongue, he is "able to keep his whole body in check." To make this point he referred to the fact that we can "put bits into the mouths of horses to make them obey us." When we do, "we can turn the *whole animal*" (Jas. 3:2-3).

I remember my first experience attending a polo match. I was awestruck at the unified effort between horse and rider. And, of course, the bit in each horse's mouth became a significant means whereby each player could control his animal.

James also illustrated the power of the tongue by referring to large ships that "are driven by strong winds." Though huge and subject to tremendous pressures, they can be "steered by a very small rudder wherever the pilot wants to go" (3:3-4).

James then made the application. "Likewise," he concluded, "the tongue is a small part of the body, but it makes great boasts" (3:5a).

On the surface it may sound as if this is a critical statement. In actuality, James was saying that the tongue is powerful. Though it is very small, it can control the whole body. If a Christian uses his tongue appropriately, he is "able to keep his whole body in check"—just as a bit can control a large horse and a small rudder can steer a huge ship.

A NEGATIVE PERSPECTIVE (James 3:5b-8)

The Tongue Can Be Powerful for Evil (James 3:5b-6)

James has told us the tongue can be a powerful force for good. It can help us become mature in Jesus Christ and give us control over our total life. But it can also be a powerful force for evil.

Again, James used an illustration. "Consider what a great forest is set on fire by a small spark," he wrote. Then he immediately made the application! "The tongue also is a fire, a world of evil among the parts of the body. It corrupts the whole person, sets the whole course of his life on fire, and is itself set on fire by hell" (3:5b-6).

If you've ever experienced a forest fire you know how ominous and frightful it can be. Out of control, it is one of the most destructive forces on earth. It literally destroys everything in its path, leaving a dismal trail of barren soil, charred trees, and homeless people and wildlife. Yet, many forest fires are started by a single spark—generated from a live coal left from a campfire or a carelessly thrown cigarette butt.

James's point is clear. The tongue is also small, but it can start a raging fire of rumor that leaves in its path devastated and disillusioned people. In some instances, it takes years to undo what is done by a carelessly spoken word.

I'm reminded of the story of a farmer's wife who had spread a slanderous story about another Christian in the village in which she lived. Soon the whole countryside had heard it. Some time later the woman became sick and confessed the story was untrue. After her recovery she came to the person she had slandered and asked his pardon. The Christian responded, "Of course I will pardon you, if you will comply with a wish of mine."

"Gladly," replied the woman.

"Go home then," said the Christian, "kill a black hen, pluck the feathers, and put them in a basket and bring them here." In half an hour the woman was back. "Now," said the Christian, "go through the village and at each street corner scatter a few of these feathers. Then take the remaining ones to the top of the bell tower of the church and scatter them to the winds." She did so, and when she returned the Christian said, "Now go through the village and gather the feathers again, and see that not one is missing."

The woman looked at the Christian in astonishment and said, "Why that is impossible! The wind has scattered them over the fields everywhere!"

"And so," said the Christian, "while I forgive you gladly, do not forget that you can never undo the damage your untrue words have done."

This is the message of James. The tongue can do irreparable damage. God forgives—and so do people. And we should forgive, no matter what the hurt. But there are some things that can never be undone completely. The scars may last a lifetime.

We Cannot Tame the Tongue by Ourselves (James 3:7-8)

Is the tongue tameable? Can we control it? The answer is yes! But it is difficult—and unpredictable. Again James illustrated. He reminded his readers that "all kinds of animals, birds, reptiles and creatures of the sea are being tamed and have been tamed by man, but," he continued, "no man can tame the tongue." The reason? "It is a restless evil, full of deadly poison" (Jas. 3:7-8).

Knowing this about the tongue, it should not surprise us that so much damage has been done through careless words, statements, or insensitive comments. This is particularly true in the lives of Christians who are not allowing themselves to be controlled by the Holy Spirit and the indwelling Christ. Satan himself is the source of this evil and his desire is to use our tongues—yes, a Christian's tongue—to hinder God's work. And the easiest way to hinder God's work is to hurt God's people.

I've been personally involved in situations where I've had to trace down a rumor, spending hours or even days unraveling the problem—only to find out what was said was either stated carelessly or misinterpreted by someone else. Think of how profitably that time could have been used to minister to people's needs, to make encouraging phone calls, to visit people who were ill, etc. How tragic when Satan scores this kind of victory—all because of a tongue out of control.

And think of those who get hurt in the process. I've known people who have been deeply wounded and have spent sleepless nights because someone has been unjustly critical. Or, if they had some justification for what they said, the *way* they said it was just as hurtful as if it had been a false judgment. This is indeed what James was referring to. The tongue can be like "deadly poison."

Consistency Is a True Test of Our Christian Maturity (James 3:9-12)

There is one sure test of the kind of relationship we have with Jesus Christ. If we "praise our Lord and Father" in one breath, and "curse men, who have been made in God's likeness," with the other, we are not walking according to God's will. We are not controlled by His Holy Spirit. We are controlled by our carnal nature. "My brothers," James wrote, "this should not be."

Again James drew from the world of nature to make his point. It is impossible for both "fresh water" and "salt water" to flow from the same source. Furthermore, it is impossible for a "fig tree" to bear olives or for a "grapevine" to bear figs. Just so, James was saying, it is not possible for praise and cursing to come from the same mouth—*if* that individual is a mature Christian.

A LARGER PERSPECTIVE

James made it clear that how we use our tongue is directly related to a Christian's level of maturity. Paul, however, gave us some additional insights. When presenting a profile for Christian maturity, particularly for men in his pastoral letters to Timothy and Titus, he began with an overarching concept: "above reproach." It is significant that this quality appears at the top of both lists (see fig. 1). Being "above reproach" certainly does not mean being perfect in every respect; rather it refers to having a "good reputation." Note, however, that the next quality listed in both passages is also the same: to be "the husband of one wife," or more literally, to be a "man of one woman."

It was very common in the first century pagan world for men to have more than one woman in their lives. Wives were primarily to oversee the home and to bear children to continue the family name. The other women were for "fun and games." For example, well-to-do men would support and visit a prostitute regularly down at the local pagan temple. In addition, he would have access to a slave girl in his own home. His wife, of course, knew all about it. There was really nothing she could do but accept this reality. It was part of the pagan culture as it is in other parts of the world, even today.

When the gospel penetrated this wicked society, it brought with it a whole new system of morality, particularly in the area of marriage and family. The "other girls" had to go. To be true to God's laws, a man was to have only one woman in his life—his wife.

1 Timothy 3:2	Titus 1:6
1. Above reproach	1. Above reproach
2. Husband of one wife	2. Husband of one wife

REPUTATION

Figure 1

1 Timothy 3:11	Titus 2:3-5
1. Worthy of respect	1. Reverent in the way they live
2. Not malicious talkers	2. Not to be slanderers

REPUTATION

Figure 2

Thus, Paul, in outlining the qualifications for an elder (which is in reality a profile for Christian maturity for all Christians), listed "husband of one wife" immediately following the quality of being "above reproach." This is true in both passages. In other words, Paul was stating that the most significant way to reflect the life-style of Jesus Christ and have a good reputation was to be *morally pure.*

Though what Paul wrote in these passages is applicable to all Christians, it is clear that what he was saying had a special application to men. Just so, he listed in the same letters some qualities that are particularly meaningful to women. (Note 1 Tim. 3:11 and Titus 2:3-5 and see figure 2.)

In his letter to Timothy, Paul stated that Christian women should be "worthy of respect." In his letter to Titus, he said that they should be "reverent in the way they live." If you study these concepts carefully you will see that they are really synonymous in meaning.

However, what is more significant is that the next quality listed in 1 Timothy 3:11 is that these women should not be "malicious talkers" and in the passage written to Titus, he said these women are "not to be slanderers." Again, we see concepts that are synonymous in meaning.

What is Paul saying? It seems he is suggesting that one of the primary areas in which a man is vulnerable is sexual. To maintain a good reputation in the Christian community, Paul implied a man must guard against impurity and immorality.

On the other hand, Paul implied that a woman's greatest area of vulnerability is in what she says. To maintain a good reputation in the Christian community, Paul was saying a woman must guard against gossip and hurtful talk.

This does not mean that both men and women are not vulnerable in both areas. Paul certainly acknowledged that. And experience verifies it. In the same passages directed to men he warned against being "quick-tempered," and "overbearing" (Titus 1:7), "violent" and "quarrelsome" (1 Tim. 3:3). And he also warned women in the passages directed to them to be "trustworthy in everything" (1 Tim. 3:11), "self-controlled and pure" (Titus 2:5). Thus, all Christians—both men and women—must be on guard against wrong use of the tongue *and* immoral behavior. But each of us has our own area of vulnerability—and we must be on guard against Satan's efforts to trip us up.

THREE WAYS TO MISUSE THE TONGUE

There are at least three ways for a Christian to misuse the tongue.

The first way to misuse the tongue is with malice. This is what James was talking about. Malicious gossip is consciously and deliberately hurtful. It is based in envy and rooted in flagrant selfishness. It is designed to destroy relationships and break up friendships.

The second way to misuse the tongue is to rationalize. This process is far more subtle than malicious use of the tongue. What makes rationalization so dangerous is that it often results from self-deception. It is rooted and based in the same motives as malicious gossip, but the person who rationalizes has become convinced that his or her motive for sharing is for "the good" of the other person or more generally, "the good" of God's work. It may be disguised as "prayer interest" or "personal concern." Nevertheless, this type of communication can be very destructive, even, in some instances, more so than malicious talk.

The third way to misuse the tongue is somewhat "innocent." This involves the individual who truly is concerned, but who is *unwise* and *insensitive* to other people's feelings. Innocent gossip is sometimes motivated by a desire to be "helpful," but in reality, the gossiper may be trying to prove to others how helpful he or she really is. In this situation there is a fine line between selfish and unselfish motives. All of us must be aware of this kind of misuse of the tongue.

A PERSONAL RESPONSE

How would you classify your use of the tongue?

	Never	Little	Sometimes	Frequently
Malicious gossip	☐	☐	☐	☐
Rationalization and self-deceptive gossip	☐	☐	☐	☐
Innocent gossip	☐	☐	☐	☐

To check your "maturity level," it is probably true that most of us engage in both a little or some self-deceptive gossip as well as innocent gossip. Our goal, of course, should be to eliminate this from our life-style; however, we'll never be able to do that completely. We must remember what James said: "We all stumble in many ways. If anyone is ***never*** at fault in what he says, he is a perfect man, able to keep his whole body in check" (Jas. 3:2). On the other hand James had already stated earlier in his letter: "If anyone considers himself religious and yet does not keep a tight rein on his tongue, he deceives himself and his religion is worthless" (1:26).

One of the greatest lessons I learned was from a woman I came to admire greatly, Dr. Henrietta Mears. She's now in heaven, but while on earth God used her greatly to touch many lives—including men like Billy Graham and Bill Bright and numerous others. In fact, Dr. Graham stated that Henrietta Mears impacted his life more than any other woman outside of his mother. And it was Dr. Mears who encouraged Bill Bright to launch the great Campus Crusade ministry in her home just off the UCLA campus.

I was privileged to be in a meeting one day with Dr. Mears. The people present were employed by her own organization, which she launched to publish Christian literature. At that time there were some things happening in the world of Christian publishing that led to some accusations and counter-accusations among various groups. Naturally and spontaneously, the subject came up for discussion among various members of the group and soon turned critical.

I'll never forget Dr. Mears's response. Immediately, she took control of the meeting, which was her prerogative, and admonished the whole group. "In our organization," she said, "we do not need to say critical things about our competitors. There's room in this world for both of us. The work of God is too great and the opportunities too numerous to be competitors. We must work together, not against each other. Furthermore," she said, "we're brothers and sisters in Christ and we shouldn't be critical of each other."

You could have heard a pin drop. Message received! And the conversation became positive rather than negative. There was great respect for this woman. She lived what she believed. That was the kind of woman Dr. Mears was. She was too great a Christian to allow herself to put others down. And she was too great a Christian leader to allow others in her organization to do the same.

I'll never forget that lesson. Though I was just a young Christian beginning in Christian ministry, I felt the impact in my life. Though I've not always been able to live out that standard in my life, with God's help I've set it as a goal. What about you?

Note

1. *The Measure of a Christian, James 1,* presents an exposition of James 1, which also deals with the problem of the tongue (Jas. 1:19-20).

4

HEAVENLY WISDOM vs. EARTHLY WISDOM

James 3:13-18

Who is wise and understanding among you? Let him show it by his good life, by deeds done in the humility that comes from wisdom. But if you harbor bitter envy and selfish ambition in your hearts, do not boast about it or deny the truth. Such "wisdom" does not come down from heaven but is earthly, unspiritual, of the devil. For where you have envy and selfish ambition, there you find disorder and every evil practice.

But the wisdom that comes from heaven is first of all pure; then peace loving, considerate, submissive, full of mercy and good fruit, impartial and sincere. Peacemakers who sow in peace raise a harvest of righteousness. (James 3:13-18)

Someone has wisely written:

A wise old owl sat in an oak;
The more he saw, the less he spoke;
The less he spoke, the more he heard;
Let's try to imitate that old bird.

Since James liked animal stories to illustrate spiritual truth, I think he would have enjoyed this bit of poetry. It summarizes the answer to his opening question in this passage on the subject of wisdom. "Who is wise and understanding among you?" he asked. In other words, what is a true test in determining if a person is wise and understanding?

James answered this question emphasizing that wisdom is not so much revealed by what we *say* as by what we *are* and what we *do*. Thus he wrote: "Let him show it"—that is, wisdom and understanding—"by his good life, by deeds done in the humility that comes from wisdom" (Jas. 3:13).

Don't misunderstand. Wisdom cannot be communicated without words. However, "words" can be meaningless if they are not validated by a demonstration of wisdom in our total life-style.

Keep in mind the context leading up to James's question in verse 13. He had just warned against being too eager to become teachers of others. Evidently there were a number of individuals in the various churches to whom James was writing who were rising up and dispensing what they felt were verbal "gems" and "pearls" of wisdom. In the process they were allowing their tongues to utter words that were unwise and that revealed a very shallow perspective on spiritual truth. Furthermore, the way they lived their own lives disqualified them from trying to teach others. Thus James exhorted these Christians to demonstrate wisdom first and foremost by living exemplary lives—lives that reflected proper Christian behavior and especially a humble spirit.

In this passage James contrasted two kinds of wisdom—"earthly wisdom" and "heavenly wisdom." And in his description, he referred to the *motivation* behind each kind of wisdom, what *characterized* this wisdom, the *source* of each kind, and the *result* when each kind was expressed. And since "earthly wisdom" seemed to be more prominent in these New Testament churches than "heavenly wisdom," that's what James described first in his letter.

EARTHLY WISDOM
(James 3:14-16)

Its Motivation (James 3:14a)

What generates "earthly wisdom"? Why is it expressed? James noted two basic reasons: "bitter envy" and "selfish ambition" (Jas. 3:14).

"Bitter envy" refers to *jealousy* that leads to anger and resentment. It can become a powerful force within an individual, leading to all kinds of irresponsible statements and actions. It is the kind of "spark" that can start a "forest fire" and do irreparable damage to others (13:5-6).

The temptation towards jealousy is no respecter of persons. F.B. Meyer, a great preacher and author, once confessed his own weakness in this area. Speaking of another great minister, he said, "It was easy to pray for the success of G. Campbell Morgan when he was in America. But when he came back to England and took a church near to mine, it was something different. The old Adam in me was inclined to jealousy, but I got my heel upon his head, and whether or not I felt right towards my friend, I determined to act right."

And F.B. Meyer *did* act right towards his fellow minister. He had his church give a special reception for G. Campbell Morgan, welcoming him to the community. And in doing so Meyer showed that he not only found himself doing the right thing, but his feelings of jealousy were dissipated. And God also honored F.B. Meyer's ministry. There were always more people to minister to than either could accommodate.

Had F.B. Meyer resorted to "earthly wisdom," he could have disqualified himself from the ministry. Jealousy is a withering emotion and ultimately destroys the very thing we're attempting to hold on to.

Selfish ambition is a related motive. It not only reflects "jealousy" but it causes a person to push himself into a position of prominence for self-centered reasons. Unfortunately, our own society condones and promotes this kind of behavior. In fact, some people of renown openly advocate it as right, proper, and necessary. For example, Merv Anderson, reviewing Dr. Hans Selve's book, *Stress Without Distress,* states that this author prescribes "a strong dose of selfishness as the best way of achieving a happier, saner society." "Unbridled idealism," he suggests, "is a cancerous curse." He even dares to attack one of the Bible's most celebrated injunctions: "Thou shalt love thy neighbor as thyself." He brands this as "biological heresy."

Dr. Selve asserts that true self-interest covers the full range of biological drives, and this includes man's social nature and his need to get along with other people.

His solution? Altruistic egotism! This is simply a case of helping others for the selfish motive of deserving help in return.

Again, this reflects the wisdom of this world. Dr. Henrietta Mears's solution to this problem reflects biblical wisdom. She wrote: "The man who keeps busy helping the man below him won't have time to envy the man above him—and there may not be anybody above him anyway."

Its Characteristics (James 3:14)

James next dealt with the characteristics of "earthly wisdom." *First, it's prideful.* It reflects arrogance. "But if you harbor bitter envy and selfish ambition in your hearts, do not *boast* about it" wrote James (3:14).

The basic Greek word used here actually means to

"boast over wrong; to be proud in spite of wrong." This, of course, is the worst kind of arrogance.

Once again, pride is no respecter of persons. One of Spurgeon's ministerial students went into the pulpit with every expression of confidence, but he had an extremely difficult time in his delivery. Afterwards he was very distressed, almost brokenhearted, and he went to Spurgeon about it. "What's wrong?" he asked this old master of homiletics and preaching. "I was prepared and felt very self-confident. I just knew I was going to do well."

Spurgeon responded, "Young man, if you'd gone up into the pulpit as you came down, you would have come down as you went up."

This story, of course, demonstrates that even those who are called of God to dispense the wisdom of God can fall into the trap of being controlled by the wisdom of this world. This was a major concern in the heart and mind of James as he wrote this letter.

Second, the wisdom of this world is characterized by dishonesty. Thus James wrote, "Do not boast about it or *deny the truth*" (3:14).

Outright, conscious lying permeated the New Testament world. Unfortunately, not all Christians overcame this habit when they put their faith in Jesus Christ. Thus Paul had to write to the Ephesians and tell them to "put off falsehood and speak truthfully to [your] neighbor" (4:25).

Unfortunately, outright lying also permeates our own society, particularly among people who are caught up in jealousy and selfish ambition. And if we are not careful, this reflection of worldly wisdom can carry over into our Christian life-style.

There is, however, a more subtle form of lying. It is self-deceptive and grows naturally out of pride. When caught in a difficult situation that is embarrassing or threatening, it is easy to rationalize, and before we know what has happened we have twisted the truth. I've caught myself in that trap. In retrospect I've had to acknowledge to myself and others that what I said did not reflect the facts. When this kind of thing happens, I can usually trace it back to some kind of fear of failure—which in itself is a subtle form of pride. Has that ever happened to you?

Its Source (James 3:15)

James next specified the source of earthly wisdom. It "does not come down from heaven," he wrote, "but is *earthly, unspiritual,* of the *devil*" (Jas. 3:15).

Not everything on earth is evil. But everything on earth is affected by evil. The sin principle is operative throughout the universe. When Satan led Adam and Eve to sin, the whole world was affected. Therefore, the wisdom of this world has as its ultimate source, Satan himself.

Its Results (James 3:16)

What happens when the wisdom of this world is operative through people? James's answer is clear and concise. "For where you have envy and selfish ambition," he wrote, "there you find disorder and every evil practice" (Jas. 3:16).

Lack of unity and harmony among people always results when the wisdom of this world is practiced. It is predictable! Envy and selfish ambition always generate antagonism, disharmony, and even chaos. And among Christians, it is Satan's greatest trick. He knows only too well the power of oneness and unity among Christians in achieving God's purposes in this world. He is keenly aware of the fact that Jesus Christ prayed for this quality among His people (John 17). And he will stop at nothing to destroy unity in order to keep people from coming to know God through Jesus Christ who, indeed, was one with the Father.

HEAVENLY WISDOM (James 3:13,17)

James next turned his attention to "the wisdom that comes from heaven."

Its Motivation (James 3:13)

Though James is not as specific in this particular passage in outlining the motive behind heavenly wisdom, the motive is a *desire to obey the will of God.* It is rooted in a commitment to practicing the truth of God.

Ultimately, of course, the motivation to practice heavenly wisdom comes from the person of the Holy Spirit and the word of God itself. It is only as we rely upon and commit ourselves to the indwelling Christ that we will be able to practice righteousness.

James earlier referred to two basic factors.

First, he spoke of being born again. God "chose to give us birth through the word of truth," he wrote (Jas. 1:18). In other words, conversion to Jesus Christ is basic to having heavenly wisdom. In this experience, Jesus Christ regenerates our hearts and gives us the capacity to think and practice God's will.

Second, James exhorted these believers to "humbly accept the word planted in you" (1:21). This, James said, "can save you"—not in terms of salvation, but in terms of persevering and living for Christ as we should. Thus Paul wrote to the Colossians, "Let the word of Christ dwell in you richly as you teach and admonish one another *with all wisdom* . . . And whatever you do, whether in word or deed, do it all in the name of the Lord Jesus, giving thanks to God the Father through him" (Col. 3:16-17).

Its Characteristics (James 3:17)

James next outlined how we can recognize wisdom from heaven.

Purity: James introduced this quality with the phrase "first of all." This indicates that purity is the most basic characteristic of heavenly wisdom. James listed it first because it belongs first. It is foundational to all the other characteristics.

When we think of being "pure," we usually think of outward acts. However, James was thinking far more deeply. His statement correlates with what Jesus said one day on a mountainside while teaching His disciples, "Blessed are the *pure in heart*" (Matt. 5:8).

James, as Jesus, was referring to an inner purity that affects everything we do. If we have not experienced change in our inner being, we will never be able to live a consistent Christian life. The harder we try to reform ourselves from without, the more we will fail and the greater the disappointment and discouragement each time it happens. Godly wisdom flows from a heart that has been indwelt and transformed by the Lord Jesus Christ.

A young man was involved in a Bible study where he was studying the beatitudes in the book of Matthew. When he was asked which of the things mentioned there would he like to have most, he said, "A pure heart." When asked why he preferred that particular quality, he responded, "If my heart were pure, I believe I would have all the other virtues mentioned by Jesus." And he was right. That is what James means when he wrote, "But the wisdom that comes from heaven is *first of all* pure" (Jas. 3:17).

James then follows this basic quality with seven more characteristics of heavenly wisdom. If it is "first of all pure," it will then be "peace loving, considerate, submissive, full of mercy and good fruit, impartial, and sincere" (3:17).

Peace loving: Christians who reflect this quality stand out in contrast to those who are divisive and who create "disorder." Peace-loving people go out of their way to create unity, to communicate clearly, to correct their mistakes. They "make every effort to keep the unity of the Spirit through the bond of peace" (Eph. 4:3).

Note! This does not mean that a Christian should maintain peace at any cost. There are some people who compromise true biblical convictions to create harmony. Jesus demonstrated that there is a time to take a stand and let the chips fall where they may. Unfortunately, some Christians "take a stand," not reflecting pure motives that flow from a pure heart, but rather their stand is motivated by "jealousy" and "selfish ambition." This is not a reflection of heavenly wisdom but earthly wisdom.

One yardstick we can use to determine our motives is the extent to which we are out of harmony with the thinking of mature Christian people who have demonstrated that maturity over the long haul—in the church, in their families, in their business life, and in their personal lives. If we *stand alone* in our disagreements, or if we stand with those who have not demonstrated good wisdom as Christians, we can be quite sure we are not thinking clearly. Our reactions are no doubt subjective and based upon motives that are more self-centered than God-centered.

Considerate: The next word James used to describe people who reflect heavenly wisdom is "considerate." In some respects it's difficult to find English words to define the real meaning inherent in this word used in the Greek New Testament. Some use the word "gentle" or "tolerant" or "equitable."

The best way to get at the meaning of this word is to think of a Christian you admire greatly, perhaps more than anyone else, for his consistent life-style and, particularly, his concern for people. As I reflected, one person instantly came to mind. He is a Christian gentleman who is over ninety years old. He is my uncle—a man who married my dad's sister. It seems the older Uncle Joe gets, the more sensitive and more tender he becomes.

One day, Elaine and I had the opportunity to fellowship with him at a Bible conference where I spoke. He made a special effort to drive over sixty miles to be with us and hear me speak. I was deeply honored. As we sat at dinner together that evening, reflecting on days gone by, his eyes often filled with tears. It was particularly true as he shared about his relationship with his wife who had gone home to be with the Lord several years before.

Aunt Hulda had a lot of difficult days before she died. And every day Uncle Joe tenderly cared for her in those final years. Physically she was unable to help herself. Consequently, he had to do everything for her. He bathed her, helped her care for her personal needs, cooked her meals, and served her faithfully until the day she died. And yet today he has only pleasant memories of their life together and his love for God has increased with the years. He is probably one of the most considerate men I know, particularly in view of his age. He is a real model of gentle, unselfish love. I could only pray that I might grow old as graciously as he has.

Submissive: Wisdom from above is also reflected in a "*submissive*" spirit. Have you ever met someone who is unusually defensive, resistant, and ready to defy any kind of authority? He appears to be constantly suspicious that someone is going to have more authority than he has. When asked to do something he almost automatically bristles. The very word *submissive* creates a negative reaction. The concept, of course, has been terribly abused and misused, which explains some negative reactions.

Godly wisdom is submissive. It is not naive, of course. It doesn't cause a person to "lie down" and say, "walk on me." But submissiveness does reflect that unique balance of being teachable and having an open heart and a willingness to serve others rather than ourselves.

Merciful and fruitful: Heavenly wisdom is also *"full of mercy and good fruit."* It is one thing to show mercy and demonstrate care and concern to someone who has suffered severe setbacks and problems. And we should. But here James was talking about being sensitive and loving towards people who have gotten themselves into trouble because of their own irresponsibility. That is the true test of whether or not "heavenly wisdom" characterizes our lives. How easy it is to say, "You got yourself into this mess—now get yourself out of it."

Realize, of course, there are people who need to pay the consequences for their actions. They will never learn otherwise. For example, the Scriptures say that "a hot-tempered man must pay the penalty; if you rescue him, you will have to do it again" (Prov. 19:19). Though this has to do with the results of irresponsible anger, the principle also applies to other areas of life. On the other hand Christians must always be ready to reach out and help a person who is in trouble, no matter what the cost. It takes wisdom of course, to know just how much to do for the individual so that on the one hand he is able to cope with the problem, but at the same time not be tempted to take advantage of the situation.

Impartial and sincere: Finally, heavenly wisdom is "impartial" and "sincere." It reflects consistency in our Christian experience.

The story is told of the Duke of Wellington that once, when he took communion at his parish church, a poor old man went up the opposite aisle. When he reached the communion table he knelt down close by the side of the Duke. Someone came and touched the old man on the shoulder and whispered to him to move farther away or to rise and wait until the Duke had received the bread and cup. However, the great commander noticed what was happening. He reached out and clasped the old man's hand

and held him to prevent him from rising. In a distant tone reflecting impartiality and sincerity, he said, "Do not move, we are all equal here." This indeed is a reflection of heavenly wisdom.

Its Source

The source of "heavenly wisdom" is God Himself. It's at this point that *motivation* and *source* overlap. No person can reflect these characteristics without knowing God personally through Jesus Christ and allowing the Holy Spirit to take control of his or her life.

Earlier James also made it very clear how a Christian can get wisdom. He wrote, "If any of you lacks wisdom, he should ask God, who gives generously to all without finding fault, and it will be given to him" (Jas. 1:5). However, we must ask in faith. Furthermore, we must ask in the context of having decided to serve Jesus Christ and Jesus Christ alone. If we are still "double-minded" and "unstable" and undecided relative to our allegiance, God does not promise to give us this kind of wisdom. God's wisdom is available. But God has specified the conditions by which we receive it.

Its Results (James 3:18)

Godly wisdom produces an atmosphere of peace and unity among believers. And, in turn, that kind of environment produces a harvest of righteousness—not unrighteousness.

Note the contrast between the *results* of "earthly" wisdom and the *results* of "heavenly" wisdom. Earthly wisdom produces *"disorder";* heavenly wisdom produces *"peace."* Earthly wisdom produces *"every evil practice";* heavenly wisdom produces a *"harvest of righteousness"* (Jas. 3:15-16,18).

A SUMMARY AND PERSONAL RESPONSE

Using the four scales, from 1 to 10 rate yourself as to *motivation, characteristics, source,* and *results.* If you fall below 5, you are moving in the direction of being controlled by "earthly wisdom." If you rate above 5, you are moving in the direction of being controlled by "heavenly wisdom." If you rate a 5, perhaps you are a "double-minded" person. You really don't know where you stand. And, of course, if you give yourself a 10, you are already in heaven! No Christian has reached perfection in this area of his life.

NOTE: All of us need to grow in wisdom and in the knowledge of our Lord Jesus Christ no matter what our age—chronologically or spiritually and no matter what our vocation and status in life.

A story is told of two ducks and a frog that lived in a certain pond on one of the farms in the East. They were the best of friends. All day long they played together. But as the hot summer days came, the pond began to dry up and soon there was so little water that they all realized that they would have to move. The ducks, of course, could easily fly to another place, but what about their friend the frog?

Finally, after a long discussion, the ducks decided to each take one end of a stick in their bills and the frog could hang onto the stick with his mouth and they would fly him to another pond. So they did.

As they were flying, a farmer out in his field looked up and saw them and said, "Well, isn't that a clever idea! I wonder who thought of it!"

The frog, as he was flying high overhead, opened his mouth and said, "I did . . . " Obviously, the frog learned a hard lesson. To paraphrase the Apostle Paul. "Let him who thinks he flies, take heed lest he crash and burn."

James asked, "Who is wise and understanding among

EARTHLY WISDOM		*HEAVENLY WISDOM*
Envy/jealousy Selfish ambition	-Motivation- 1 2 3 4 5 6 7 8 9 10	Conversion to Christ Desire to do will of God
Pride Dishonesty	-Characteristics- 1 2 3 4 5 6 7 8 9 10	Pure Peace loving Considerate Submissive Full of Mercy and good fruit Impartial and sincere
Satan Self	-Source- 1 2 3 4 5 6 7 8 9 10	God Jesus Christ Holy Spirit The Scriptures
Disorder Every evil practice	-Results- 1 2 3 4 5 6 7 8 9 10	Peace Righteousness

you? Let him *show it*" (3:13). The frog made a fatal mistake when he tried to *say* it. But he made a worse mistake when he allowed pride to cause him to take all the credit himself. Thus he violated a second principle manifesting wisdom. What we do is to be "done in *humility* that comes from wisdom."

A PRAYER

Father, I confess I cannot reflect heavenly wisdom in my own strength. First of all I need a changed heart. Second, I need a heart that is dedicated and devoted to you. Dear Jesus, I receive you as my Saviour from sin and commit my heart and life to you to live your life in and through me. In Jesus' name. Amen.

5

FRIEND OF THE WORLD! ENEMY OF GOD!

James 4:1-6a

What causes fights and quarrels among you? Don't they come from your desires that battle within you? You want something but don't get it. You kill and covet, but you cannot have what you want. You quarrel and fight. You do not have, because you do not ask God. When you ask, you do not receive, because you ask with wrong motives, that you may spend what you get on your pleasures.

You adulterous people, don't you know that friendship with the world is hatred toward God? Anyone who chooses to be a friend of the world becomes an enemy of God. Or do you think Scripture says without reason that the spirit he caused to live in us tends toward envy, but he gives us more grace? (James 4:1-6a)

Some preachers, like pilots, circle the field about ten times before they land. Not James! He consistently made a three-point landing on the first approach! Throughout his letter, James wasted no time or words in coming straight to the point.

However, James used a rather subtle and sensitive communication technique—a series of questions. He often asked his audience to think about an issue before he gave a specific answer.

This technique first appears when James addressed the subject that might be classified as the theme in this letter. Note the following pattern—including the question introducing the paragraph we want to consider in this chapter.

THE ISSUES	*THE QUESTIONS*	*THE ANSWERS*
WORKS	"What good is it, my brothers, if a man claims to have faith but has no deeds?" (2:14)	"Faith by itself, if it is not accompanied by action, is dead" (2:17)
WISDOM	"Who is wise and understanding among you?" (3:13a)	"Let him show it by his good life, by deeds done in the humility that comes from wisdom" (3:13b)
WORLD-LINESS	"What causes fights and quarrels among you?" (4:1a)	"Don't they come from your desires that battle within you?" (4:1b)

"YOU QUARREL AND FIGHT" (James 4:1)

Some of these believers were involved in some "heavy duty" arguments, so much so that James used some strong words to describe what was happening. The two words he used—"fights" and "quarrels"—appear together frequently in ancient Greek literature, such as in Homer and Plato. They were used to describe battles of every kind—battles of words; legal battles; and outright war.

These Christians were probably not engaged in actual battles resulting in physical harm. However, in their own way they were in a "state of war," involving a continuous state of unrest and tension as well as periodic skirmishes.[1]

How can this be? What was happening? Can people who claim to be followers of Jesus Christ actually wage war on one another?

Christianity Today once reported on a twentieth-century church in Wichita, Kansas, that was so out of control that on several occasions the local police had to step in to restore order. The trouble apparently stemmed from a battle over control of the church—a so-called "Christian church."

Is it possible for Christians to "fight" and "quarrel"? Let me use James's technique. Is it possible for members of a Christian family to "fight" and "quarrel"? Most of us know families that are in a constant state of tension. In some instances not a day goes by but there are either minor or major blow-ups. It's sad but true! Unfortunately this kind of quarreling and fighting can spill over into the larger Christian family—the church. And when it does, it is a great contradiction to all that Jesus Christ stands for. And when it becomes an open issue, it represents a great victory for Satan.

What Was Causing This Tension? (James 4:1)

James's initial question to these first-century Christians explored what was causing these fights and quarrels. His answer focused on what he identified as "desires" that were battling within them (Jas. 4:1b). In other words, there was a war going on inside these believers' lives which was working its way to the outside.

The Greek word translated "desires" in this verse is *heedonai,* from which we get our English word "hedonism." In many respects it is a synonym to another word, *epithumeite,* that is also translated "desire"—such as the word used earlier by James when he wrote about temptation.[2] "Each one is tempted," he wrote, "when, by his own *evil desire,* he is dragged away and enticed. Then, after *desire* has conceived, it gives birth to sin; and sin, when it is full-grown, gives birth to death" (1:14-15).

Heedonai, the word James used in James 4:1, though very similar in meaning to the word he used earlier in chapter 1, refers to *desire that has become actualized.* It is more than a desire to have or do something; it involves the *pleasure* that accompanies the desire. In many respects it is "desire" that "has conceived" and has already "given birth to sin."

In the ancient Greek world, a man by the name of Aristippus introduced the concept of *hedonism*—a philosophy that teaches that pleasure in people is good and should be sought and nurtured, while any kind of pain involves evil and should be avoided. Socrates and Plato, also Greek philosophers, took issue with this approach to life. They believed that the highest goal in life should be good—not pleasure per se. It is understandable why the biblical writers would align themselves more with Plato and Socrates.

In the twentieth-century world, hedonism is often identified with the "playboy"—and in more recent years, the "playgirl" philosophy of life. Though it includes a whole range of "pleasures," it most frequently focuses on sexual activity.

"YOU KILL AND COVET" (James 4:2)

What was happening in these first-century churches? "You want something," James wrote, "but don't get it." Then what? "You kill and covet," James continued, "but you cannot have what you want." The result? James then restated the outward manifestation of the problem—"You quarrel and fight!" (Jas. 4:2).

When Is "Desire" and "Pleasure" Sinful?

Before analyzing the problem further in these New Testament churches, it is important to differentiate between what is sinful desire and pleasure, and desire and pleasure that is not sinful. Four-hundred years before Christ was born, the great Greek philosopher Plato concluded that "the sole source of wars, and revolutions, and battles is nothing other than the body and its desires."[3]

Plato was a wise man, but he was wrong when he stated that the body itself is evil. Unfortunately, some Christians concluded that the Bible was teaching the same thing as this Greek philosopher, and this led to all kinds of aesthetic practices. These believers thought that the solution to spirituality was to deprive or even mistreat their bodies and deny themselves what Paul calls the "good things" God had created for man to enjoy. Paul warned against this kind of teaching and behavior in his first letter to Timothy, tracing its source back to Satan. "They forbid people to marry," he wrote, "and order them to abstain from certain foods, which God created to be received with thanksgiving by those who believe and who know the truth." And then Paul stated a very important fact in answering the question just raised relative to when is desire and pleasure sinful. "For everything God created is good, and *nothing* is to be rejected if it is received with thanksgiving, because it is consecrated by the *word of God* and *prayer*" (1 Tim. 4:3-5).

"Desires" and "pleasures" become sinful when we violate God's revealed will in both thought and action. For example, *food is a gift of God.* To desire it is normal and to enjoy it is a blessing from God. In fact, close your eyes for a moment and think about the most delicious meal you've ever eaten. My problem is I can think of dozens! I enjoy good food. Wouldn't it be horrible to lose your appetite for food? That is, now and forever! What I do with my appetite for food, however, is *very* important.

Food in itself is not sinful. Neither is the appetite for food. However, I can eat in moderation or I can become gluttonous. And if I allow myself to become gluttonous, the Bible says I have allowed my desires to give birth to sin. I am now living to eat rather than eating to live. There *is* a difference!

Sexual appetites are also God-created and designed to give pleasure. However, we can allow these appetites to cause us to violate God's laws—both in mind and body. Inappropriately expressed outside the bonds of marriage, these appetites become sinful and selfish actions. Expressed within the bonds of marriage they become a God-created means to provide pleasure, happiness, security, and the blessing of children. If you don't believe God created sexual pleasure, read the Song of Solomon.

Sex is a powerful desire—emotionally and physically. If it were not, it would not permeate our literature, movies, and music. Unfortunately, most of what is presented today focuses on illegitimate sex—fornication, adultery, and homosexuality. It's a sad commentary on our American society. And one of the fastest ways to turn our God-created urges in evil directions is to feed our minds on sexually oriented material that is a perversion of what God intended.

But again, sexual desire and sex per se are not evil. Listen to this advice from the Word of God: "Drink water from your own cistern, running water from your own well. Should your springs overflow in the streets, your streams of water in the public squares? Let them be yours alone, never to be shared with strangers. May your fountain be blessed, and may you rejoice in the wife of your youth. A loving doe, a graceful deer—may her breasts satisfy you always, may you ever be captivated by her love. Why be captivated, my son, by an adulteress? Why embrace the bosom of another man's wife?" (Prov. 5:15-20).

Material things are also a blessing of God. Who in our society does not enjoy a nice home, a comfortable car, a week at the beach or on the ski slopes? Is this sinful? Of course not—unless it becomes central in our lives. When material blessings are used selfishly and draw our hearts away from God rather than towards God, we allow our desires to give birth to sin.

Interestingly, when all of the above-mentioned blessings are abused, misused, and allowed to become a means to sin, they never satisfy. Dr. Samuel Johnson, an eighteenth-century scholar, once wrote: "All that have tried the selfish experiment, let one come forth and say that he has succeeded. He that has made gold his idol, has it satisfied him? He that has toiled in the fields of ambition, has he been repaid? He that has ransacked every theatre of sensual enjoyment, is he content? Can any answer in the affirmative? Not one! As John McMurray succinctly put it, 'The best cure for hedonism is the attempt to practice it.'"

This observation is verified in the Word of God itself. Solomon wrote: "I denied myself nothing my eyes desired; I refused my heart no pleasure. My heart took delight in all my work, and this was the reward for all my labor. Yet when I surveyed all that my hands had done and what I had toiled to achieve, everything was meaningless, a chasing after the wind; nothing was gained under the sun" (Eccles. 2:10-11).

Against this backdrop, we are ready to answer the question, What was happening in the churches James was addressing? They were allowing normal and natural God-created desires to "give birth to sin." Thus James wrote: "You want something but don't get it"; and then he said, "You kill and covet."

Again, these are strong words. It is doubtful that these Christians were resorting to actual murder because of their jealousy. It should be noted, however, that covetousness and jealousy are powerful desires and caused one of God's choicest servants not only to commit adultery but also to commit murder. King David violated both of these commandments of God, and though the Lord was merciful, this man after God's own heart experienced painful consequences the rest of his life.

Can this happen to a twentieth-century Christan? I personally know a married man who, a professed believer, became involved with another woman. At the instigation of his lover, he decided to kill his wife. So, unknown to her, he contracted with a man to kill her and to make her death appear as though it occurred in an attempted rape. Fortunately, the would-be killer tipped off the police and the errant husband was arrested.

Those of us who knew this brother in Christ were stunned! As a Christian, how could he resort to attempted murder? Behind the scheme was a jealous "other woman" who helped her lover engineer the plot to kill his wife, demonstrating that it can happen today—literally! Coveting can be a strong and evil desire leading to irrational behavior.

It is more likely, however, that James is using these words to describe character assassination and other sinful actions against fellow Christians. For example, they may have been jealous of one another's positions in the church and resorted to gossip in order to hurt another's reputation. There is more than one way to "commit murder," just as there is more than one way to "commit adultery."

Jesus made this point very clear (Matt. 5:21-22; 27-28). Desires can become so intense and feelings so strong that they lead to actualization in the mind and heart. When they do, in God's sight they're considered just as sinful as the overt actions themselves. This happens, of course, when we allow our desires to become evil and then to be "dragged away and enticed" (Jas. 1:14).

The story is told about a family, living in a small town in North Dakota. It was a happy little family, even though the young mother had not been entirely well since the birth of her second baby.

But each evening the neighbors' hearts warmed when they saw the husband and father being met at the gate by his wife and two small children. There was laughter in the evening too, and when the weather was nice Father and children would romp together on the back lawn while Mother looked on with happy smiles.

Then one day a village gossip started a story saying that the father was being unfaithful to his wife, a story entirely without foundation. But it eventually came to the ears of the young wife, and it was more than she could bear.

Reason left its throne, and that night when her husband came home there was no one to meet him at the gate, no laughter in the house, no fragrant aroma coming from the kitchen—only coldness and something that chilled his heart with fear.

And down in the basement he found the three of them

hanging from a beam. Sick and in despair, the young mother had first taken the lives of her two children, and then her own.

In the days that followed, the truth of what had happened came out—a gossip's tongue, an untrue story, a terrible tragedy.

How does God evaluate this kind of situation? It was murder—by a gossip's tongue!

"YOU DO NOT ASK GOD" (James 4:3-4)

These New Testament Christians had a basic problem that gave birth to the problem we've already outlined. In fact, they had two interrelated problems. When they experienced legitimate desires, they took matters into their own hands and did not consult God. Before long, they were trying to fulfill their desires in sinful ways. And when they did ask God to help them, they went about it improperly. In fact, their motives were purely selfish. They tried to manipulate God. Consequently, the Lord turned a deaf ear to their prayers (Jas. 4:3).

At this point James went straight for the jugular vein. He used his strongest words yet! He called them "adulterous people"—a phrase any Christian Jew would recognize. Frequently in the Old Testament the analogy of adultery was used to describe Israel's unfaithfulness to God. In Jeremiah 3:20 we read, "But like a woman unfaithful to her husband, so you have been unfaithful to me, O house of Israel." And in the New Testament the Church is referred to as the "bride of Christ."

The picture is clear. Many of these Christians to whom James was writing were committing "spiritual adultery." They were having a love affair with the world. Thus James asked another pointed question, "Don't you know that friendship with the world is hatred toward God?" And then comes another direct answer: "Anyone who *chooses* to be a friend of the world becomes an enemy of God" (Jas. 4:4).

Many of these believers had deliberately chosen to align themselves with the world system. They were operating with earthly wisdom rather than heavenly wisdom. Bitter "envy" and "selfish ambition" had taken over their hearts. They were boasting and denying the truth. The result was "disorder and every evil practice" (3:13-16). And thus we see the continuity between the last paragraph in chapter 3 and this first paragraph in chapter 4.

FRIEND OF GOD! ENEMY OF THE WORLD!

The New Testament world was a totally pagan culture. Materialism reigned supreme! The society in general was X-rated. Prostitution was part of their religious ritual. Human life was cheap. Divorce was rampant.

Large cities particularly were centers of debauchery. For example, Antioch—a city of nearly 500 thousand people—exemplified a social life that was debased, sensual and shocking.

Ephesus was a great pagan religious center, housing the great temple of Diana, a fertility goddess. An annual festival in her honor was held during the months of March and April. People actually worshiped Diana by means of sexual orgies and ceremonial prostitution. Fathers, mothers, and children observed and took part in these degenerate activities.

Rome, a city of nearly a million and a half people by the early part of the second century, was also well-known for its moral degradation. Stage shows featured live sexual activity and the amphitheaters featured contests between men and animals and between men and men who engaged in bloody duels that often resulted in death. In order to cater to a growing appetite for violence, the contests were planned more and more elaborately and became intensely shocking.

It was in these wicked cities that churches were planted. For the first time ever the gospel and teachings of Jesus Christ began to penetrate the pagan environment.

It is not surprising that it took time for some Christians to break away from their old habit patterns and to live for Jesus Christ. Even Jews who had been taught the Law of Moses had been so affected by the Greek and Roman life-style that they too were people in transition. Thus we can understand some of the things that were happening in the churches that James addressed in his little Epistle.

Today we see an interesting phenomenon in our own society—in some respects a reverse phenomenon. Our own nation was built on a commitment to the ethical and moral values inherent in the Hebrew/Christian tradition. Though we have never been a Christian nation in the true sense of that word, Americans, in general, have lived their lives, conducted their business, and related to their neighbors with a value system reflecting a semblance of morality, honesty, and integrity.

But all of that has changed radically in the last several decades. Our value system has changed dramatically. Unfortunately, the world's system in many respects is pressing in on the Christian community. What is openly tolerated in our society today, seen against the backdrop of twenty years ago, reveals incredible and shocking changes.

Those being affected the most are our own children. Marie Winn, by no means an evangelical writer, released a book entitled *Children Without Childhood.* She is concerned! Regarding parents, she writes: "Never in their worst fantasies did they imagine that their ten or eleven year olds might smoke dope or get involved in sexual activity or run away from home." But, she continues, parents are faced with the knowledge that their children can get involved in any number of dangerous, illegal, or merely unsuitable activities. Their children "do become potheads, do have sexual intercourse, do watch pornographic films on television." Though she says the percentage is yet small, it is happening. Of course, as the years go by, the number will increase.[4]

What has caused all this? She writes—"Children's lives are always a mirror of adult life. The great social upheavals of the late 1960's and early 1970's—the so-called sexual revolution, the women's movement, the proliferation of television in American homes and its larger role in child rearing and family life, the rapid increase in divorce and single parenthood, the political disillusionment in the Viet Nam and post-Viet Nam era, a deteriorating economic situation that propels mothers into the work force—all these brought about changes in adult life that necessitated new ways of dealing with children."[5]

Winn goes on to comment that today our children are not protected from the "secret underside" of adult lives—"adult sexuality, violence, injustice, suffering, fear of death." Consequently, "those former innocents grow tougher, perforce, less playful and trusting, more skeptical—in short, more like adults."[6]

Ms. Winn, though analyzing the situation rather accurately, does not give solutions. That is understandable! She really doesn't have any. Diane Casselberry, reviewing this book for the *Christian Science Monitor* concludes—"Some readers may protest that the book leaves them feeling somewhat helpless."[7] Frankly, if I were not a Christian, I'd feel helpless too.

But I don't! As Christians we have answers. If parents could successfully guide their children out of the moral mess that existed in the first-century world, why can we not protect our children from the world as it begins to impact our own society? We have the resources at our disposal to guide our children through these changing times.

But there is a condition. We, as adults, must be consistent in our own lives. We—to quote James—must keep ourselves "from being polluted by the world" (1:27).

One thing is certain! We will never protect our children and prepare them to live for Jesus Christ in our present society—

- If we live double lives
- If we do not communicate with words of wisdom and grace that reflect the love of Jesus Christ
- If we get caught up in materialism
- If we don't set priorities in developing a systematic program of giving and sharing our material blessings with the ministry of God
- If we indulge in adult entertainment that is illicit and immoral.
- If we are inconsistent in gathering together to worship with God's people
- If we are dishonest—even telling what we call little "white lies." For example, someone calls and you say, "Tell them I'm not home."
- If we cheat. For example, someone gives you too much change at the cash register and you keep it rather than return it.

Let us not think we can hide these facts from our children! They soon discover what is going on. And if we should succeed in hiding the fact, they'll soon see it in our own life-style. The contemporary adage is true: "Garbage In! Garbage Out!" It soon dulls our love for Jesus Christ.

There is a way to combat worldliness! That way is to be a friend of God and not a friend of the world. If we live consistent Christian lives according to the principles of Scripture, our children will grow up reflecting those principles. Even if they depart from the straight and narrow, they will be back. When the world system no longer satisfies, they will have something to return to because they have seen and experienced Christian reality.

J.A. Hadfield, a British psychologist writing several years ago, made a very perceptive observation. Even as a non-Christian he saw the impact of the modeling process on children. He wrote: "If you never taught a child one single moral maxim, he would nevertheless develop moral—or immoral—standards of right and wrong by the process of identification."[8]

This is the secret: not preaching, but practicing! We must live for Jesus Christ in all that we do and say. This is the message of James again and again.

A PRAYER FOR YOUR CHURCH

Dear Father, help us as a body of believers to live like Jesus Christ in all that we do. May we become known as a body of Christians who love God with all our hearts and our neighbors as ourselves. And this we pray for each family unit in our church. Lord, the direction of our society is scary. But thank you that we have solutions! We have your Word to guide us! We have your Spirit who lives within us to assist us! We have brothers and sisters in Christ who can help us walk through the wilderness of this life. Thank you that you have promised never to leave us or to forsake us. In Jesus' name, Amen.

A FINAL THOUGHT FROM PAUL

"For the grace of God that brings salvation has appeared to all men. It teaches us to say 'No' to ungodliness and worldly passions, and to live self-controlled, upright and godly lives in this present age, while we wait for the blessed hope—the glorious appearing of our great God and Savior, Jesus Christ" (Titus 2:11-13).

Notes

1. *Polemos,* here translated "quarrels" literally means "war"; *machee,* here translated "fight" literally means battle. *Polemos* refers to the continual state of unrest in the church; *machee* refers to the periodic skirmishes.
2. *Epithumeite* is often translated "lust" in the King James Version.
3. John Blanchard, *Not Hearers Only,* vol. 3 (London: Wordbooks, 1973), p. 20.
4. Marie Winn, *Children Without Childhood* (New York: Pantheon Books, 1983), pp. 11-12.
5. Ibid., pp. 5-6.
6. Ibid., pp. 6-7.
7. *Dallas Morning News,* August, 1983.
8. J.A. Hadfield, *Childhood and Adolescence* (Baltimore: Penguin, 1962), p. 134.

6

THE PERIL OF PRIDE
James 4:6b-10

That is why Scripture says: "God opposes the proud but gives grace to the humble." Submit yourselves, then, to God. Resist the devil, and he will flee from you. Come near to God and he will come near to you. Wash your hands, you sinners, and purify your hearts, you double-minded. Grieve, mourn and wail. Change your laughter to mourning and you joy to gloom. Humble yourselves before the Lord, and he will lift you up. (James 4:6b-10)

F.B. Meyer once wrote:

I used to think, that God's gifts were on shelves
one
above
another
and the taller we grow,
The easier to reach them.
Now I find, that
God's gifts are on shelves
one
beneath
another
and the lower we stoop,
The more we get.

Humility versus pride is a strong theme in the book of James. Thus he wrote—quoting an Old Testament proverb, "God opposes the proud but gives grace to the humble" (4:6b). To be in opposition to God is indeed a perilous position!

I'm reminded of the atheist who, attempting to demonstrate to his audience there was no God, shook his fist at the heavens, shouting, "God, if you exist, strike me dead!"

How foolish! How tragic! But how revealing! God's grace is far greater than man's stupidity, foolishness, and arrogance. Though "the fool says in his heart, 'There is no God'" (Ps. 14:1), God says, I love all people—even fools. He is longsuffering with those who deny even His existence!

But to love is to disallow manipulation. And God does not cater to the prideful. The Scriptures clearly state that He *opposes them*! And again I repeat, that is a perilous position. If I'm in opposition to the Creator of the universe, I'm on a collision course. I'm in a no-win situation. Thus James—writing to New Testament Christians, some of whom were on this collision course—shared with them some very specific instructions on how they could avoid this trap.

James's paragraph in verses 7 to 10 is in some respects difficult to teach because it contains at least seven powerful exhortations. Each could serve as the basis for a single lesson or study. On the other hand, it is helpful to understand all of these concepts both in concert and context—and particularly in the context of "pride" versus "humility."

Note that James frames this passage with this overarching concern, as illustrated in the following list:

GOD OPPOSES THE PROUD, BUT GIVES GRACE TO THE HUMBLE

1. Submit yourselves, then, to God.
2. Resist the devil, and he will flee from you.
3. Come near to God and He will come near to you.
4. Wash your hands, you sinners.
5. Purify your hearts, you double-minded.
6. Grieve, mourn and wail.
7. Change your laughter to mourning and your joy to gloom.

HUMBLE YOURSELF BEFORE THE LORD, AND HE WILL LIFT YOU UP

Although James outlined seven exhortations in this power-packed paragraph, inherent in these seven statements are three basic actions a Christian must take to overcome pride.

SUBMISSIVENESS TO GOD (James 4:7-8a)

Every Christian is tempted in the area of pride. What must we do, then, to keep pride from emerging and controlling our lives? First, James says, "*Submit* yourselves . . . to God" (4:7a). Since "God opposes the proud but gives grace to the humble," it is only logical that we do not stiffen our necks against our Creator, which is the ultimate in pride. Furthermore, to resist God cuts off His grace—the very source of strength we need to live humbly before God.

James goes on to outline two *action steps* that are necessary if we are to submit ourselves to God.

"Resist the Devil" (James 4:7)

To be submissive to God, there must be *resistance*! But, not toward God. It must be directed toward Satan—the enemy of all that is right and good.

Satan is a reality. The most important truth in the exhortation to "resist the devil" is that Satan exists! He is a created being, a powerful personality! At one time he was the most outstanding angel of God—a "model of perfection, full of wisdom and perfect in beauty" (Ezek. 28:12–13,15).

But Satan fell from this lofty position. The reason was pride. He became enamored with his own beauty and splendor (Ezek. 28:17). Eventually he wanted to be like God (Isa. 14:12-15). It should not surprise us, then, that Satan's strongest attack against a Christian is in the area of pride. He is the author of pride; it was the cause of his own downfall.

When Satan fell God did not take away his power. Furthermore, Satan is assisted in his diabolical work by an immeasurable host of demons or fallen angels who no doubt were judged with Satan when he fell from his lofty position. All of this took place in eternity past.

It is important to understand, however, that Satan *is* limited. Though more powerful than any other evil personality, he is *not omnipresent*—that is, he cannot be everywhere at the same time. Furthermore, he is *not omniscient.* Though he is very wise he doesn't know everything. And, perhaps most important, he is *not omnipotent.* His power *is* limited. Only God is characterized by these three qualities. Though Satan wanted to have these qualities, instead he brought judgment on himself.

However, we must hasten to point out that Satan exerts tremendous power throughout the world through a host of demons, those "fallen angels" that do his bidding. They form an incredible intelligence network enabling Satan to operate on the basis of a tremendous amount of knowledge.

When the Russians shot down an unarmed, commercial Korean 747 aircraft in August of 1983, taking the lives of over 250 innocent civilians, it was amazing to most Americans to gain firsthand knowledge of the intelligence network that is operative in the Western world. We were able to reconstruct what happened almost to the exact detail. If this can be achieved at a human level, think of the magnitude of Satan's intelligence network that exists in "the powers of this dark world" and within "the spiritual forces of evil in the heavenly realms" (Eph. 6:12). He is no doubt monitoring the activities of every Christian on planet Earth, particularly those who are resisting him and serving God faithfully.

Satan can be defeated. The *second* important factor in James's statement about resisting Satan is that, though he is extremely powerful, he need not overpower us and cause us to sin. As Christians we can "resist" him, and when we do, "he will flee" from us.

What does it mean to resist Satan? First, we must understand that Satan's influence is ordinarily not person to person as it was with Jesus Christ when He was tempted in the wilderness. His mode of operation is not to go around "whispering naughty thoughts" in our ears.

I remember when my son Kenton was about four years old. We were in the master bedroom. Predictably, for a four-year-old, he began using our bed as a trampoline. I told him to stop jumping—which he did for a few seconds. He then proceeded to continue jumping. I warned him a second time! And again he stopped—for a few seconds. The third time it happened, I decided that words were not working. Rather, I reached over and gave him a good swat on his you-know-what, which really shocked him. Stunned, he immediately flopped on the bed and burst into tears. (He was more shocked than hurt.)

I then decided to give him some alone-time to cry it out and develop some objectivity. I left the bedroom and went into the family room. In a couple of minutes he sheepishly made his way out to where I was. I had a little "Nerf" ball in my hand and as soon as I saw him peer around the corner, I threw it to him. He immediately caught it and threw it back, and was once again all smiles.

We continued playing catch for a few minutes—and he suddenly stopped and got very serious. "You know what, Daddy?" he said. "When you told me to stop jumping, Satan whispered in my ear and said, 'Just one more time won't matter, Kenton!' But," he said, "it did!"

Actually, I have forgotten what I said in response. Inwardly I was smiling, but I didn't show it because he was so serious. But I distinctly remember thinking that theologically he was confused regarding *how* Satan communicates.

Actually, no one was whispering in Kenton's ear—*except* Kenton. He was talking to himself and following his predictable and natural urges. It was fun to jump on our bed.

And so it is with many people. We blame Satan for putting thoughts in our heads, whereas we're simply enticed by our own desires, some of which are evil (see Jas. 1:14).

How then does Satan tempt us? It's primarily through the *effects* of sin and evil in the world. Satan's influence is all around us—in what we see and hear. All creation has been affected by his direct contact with Adam and Eve in the Garden of Eden. The principle of sin is operative everywhere.

If this is true, how do we resist Satan? Paul, as he so often does, gives us a detailed description of James's generalization (see Eph. 6:10-18). When Paul wrote to the Ephesians, he told them to "put on the full armor of God." In so doing, he wrote, we can "stand against the devil's schemes."

In this passage Paul clearly outlines what this armor is:

- The belt of truth
- The breastplate of righteousness
- The gospel of peace
- The shield of faith
- The helmet of salvation
- The sword of the Spirit, which is the Word of God
- Prayer.

To resist Satan, then, means to "stand firm" (Eph. 6:14) against his evil schemes and influences in the world. As Christians, we are participating in a one-sided game. We can always be on the offensive. We can always be marching toward the goal line. We never need to turn and run away.

If we turn and run, Satan's influence is somewhat like a barking dog. I remember one day, when I was a young boy, learning a very difficult but profitable lesson. I went to visit my cousin and, when I opened the screen door on the back porch, a little black dog approached me, barking ferociously. It scared me to death and I instinctively ran. Before I knew what happened, he caught me and sank his teeth into one of my legs.

I found out later that what happened was unusual. That dog didn't bite people. Why then did he bite me? Because I ran! I'm told that dogs sense when the object of their aggression is afraid. They can even smell it.

A Christian need not turn and run from Satan's evil influence. We can face him with courage and strength, knowing we can win *if* we put on the whole armor of God. That is what it means when James says, "Resist the devil, and he will flee from you."

One word of warning! The dog illustration has some weaknesses. If you see a sign that says: "Beware, mad dog," it would be asking for serious trouble to enter his territory. And just so with certain situations in this world—there are certain places a Christian should not go.

There are certain associations Christians must avoid. There are certain things we should not see. If we do, we are not resisting Satan. We're entering his territory with our guard down. Don't be surprised when he scores against you. Under these circumstances you may have just handed him the ball on your own ten-yard line.

"Come Near to God" (James 4:8)

The first step in *submitting* ourselves to God is to resist Satan. The second step is to "*come near* to God." And if we do, James wrote, "He will come near to you."

There are Christians who believe that God is holding them at a distance, no matter how hard they try to get close to Him. That feeling is our problem—not His. He always responds when we seek to do His will. He will not reject us.

Acts of manipulation. Unfortunately, some Christians have a false view of what it means to "come near to God." They call on Him *only* when they are in trouble. They live their lives the way they want to live them—*until* they get into trouble. Then they come to God for help. Earlier James spoke to this issue when he wrote: "When you ask, you do not receive, because you ask with wrong motives, that you may spend what you get on your own pleasures" (Jas. 4:3).

It should not surprise us that God does not respond to this kind of manipulation. That is not what James meant when he said to "come near to God." A Christian who is living close to God has developed a relationship with God. He has consistently put God first in his life.

Some Christians are like husbands who ignore their wives and live their own self-centered lives—until they want their own needs met. They then wonder why their wives do not respond to their overtures.

And the same can be said of wives who put everything

and everyone else first in their lives, until they want something to further their own selfish interests. They then wonder why their husbands are reluctant to respond to *their* desires.

James is not talking about a fickle, superficial, game-playing relationship with God. A Christian who comes close to God has offered his body to the Lord as a living sacrifice. He is not conforming any longer to the pattern of this world, but is being transformed by the renewing of his mind. And when this happens, God responds. His will becomes clear. He comes near to us.

Feelings of rejection. We must make one other important observation. Some Christians have difficulty *feeling* God's closeness because they have never felt closeness with other human beings. Their experience with authority figures in their lives has been one of conditional acceptance or even rejection. It is natural to project these feelings on God.

I remember overhearing my two daughters talking one day when they were about four and five years old. They were having a "little girl conversation," but didn't know I was listening in. Robyn, the youngest, said—with a stroke of insight, "You know, Renee, God is our heavenly Daddy."

Actually, I was jolted! It suddenly dawned on me that their view of me was their view of God. How they felt about me at that point in their lives was how they felt about God. If their relationship with me was warm and accepting, their relationship with God would *feel* warm and accepting. Conversely, if their relationship with me, their earthly father, involved emotional distance, they would feel the same about God, their heavenly Father. This, of course, indicates the importance of the father image in the home.

Christians who have experienced emotional distance,

particularly from parents, must realize that God is not ignoring them or rejecting them when they attempt to draw near to Him. They are simply projecting their own feelings on Him. In time, they can begin to feel a closeness as they come to understand their problems and as they develop warm and accepting relationships with other Christians. This, of course, demonstrates the importance of the family of God. Together, we can "reparent" one another—particularly if we love one another as Christ loved us.

BEHAVIORAL CHANGE
(James 4:8b)

The first basic action to combat pride in our lives is to submit our wills to God. The second is "behavioral change." True submission always results in a change in attitudes and actions.

James wrote about change in two areas which must always go together to reflect *real* change. The first is the *true test* of change—the *external*. The second is the *true reason* for change—the *internal*.

"Wash Your Hands"

Jewish Christians who were the original recipients of James's letter, would clearly understand this exhortation. In the Old Testament the priests had to wash their hands *and* their feet before entering the Tabernacle to worship God (Exod. 30:17-21). And the Pharisees at the time of Christ were obsessed with "hand washing" routines and ceremonies (Mark 7:3-4). To them it was a sign of cleansing.

James is not advocating continuing this Old Testament practice. Rather, he used this illustration to emphasize the fact that "resisting Satan" and "coming near to God" must be accompanied by behavioral change. This is the major theme in James's Epistle. We must turn our backs on sin. And the cleansing agent is not water—it's the blood of Jesus Christ (see 1 John 1:7).

"Purify Your Hearts"

True external change originates in the heart. James was not advocating simply turning over a *new leaf.* He was referring to change at the *root* level of life.

Many of these believers, as we've already noticed, were "double-minded." They were identifying with Christ, but in name only. They were not humbly accepting the word planted in them and allowing it to change them from the inside out (see Jas. 1:21). They were listening to the word, but not doing what it said (see 1:22). Consequently, they were "double-minded" and "unstable in all" they were doing (1:8).

GODLY SORROW (James 4:9)

There are some Christians who sin, get caught—and are sorry. But, the reason for their sorrow is that they got caught. This is *not* true repentance. And their unwillingness to be repentant also reflects pride.

The concept of repentance involves change. It literally means to do an about-face. But inherent in this process is godly sorrow.

The Christians James was addressing were living in sin and rejoicing in it. Thus James wrote, "Grieve, mourn and wail. Change your laughter to mourning and your joy to gloom" (Jas. 4:9).

The Corinthians were also guilty of this kind of behavior (see 1 Cor. 5:1-2). Paul had to deal with them severely, though he experienced a great deal of anxiety in his own heart when he had to be so blunt. But the results were positive and encouraging. The Corinthians responded with godly sorrow which led to true repentance (2 Cor. 7:8-13). This change was both internal *and* external.

Don't misunderstand! James is not teaching that Christians should be sober-faced, down-in-the-mouth people. Christians more than anyone else have the right to laugh, to rejoice, and to express happiness. But, Christians who are deliberately living in sin ought not to be laughing! They ought to be mourning. This is James's message to these New Testament Christians, many of whom were continuing in sin and reflecting a double-minded life-style.

I distinctly remember confronting a Christian with flagrant sin. He was caught in the act and admitted it. Initially there appeared to be remorse. However, the so-called "remorse" was eventually followed by anger for having been confronted.

On the basis of Scripture, what do you think? Was this person truly sorry for his sin, or was he sorry because he got caught?

The bottom line relative to what James has communicated in this brief paragraph, which is packed with eternal truth, is that the way to avoid the *peril of pride* is the process whereby we humble ourselves before the Lord. And when we do, James wrote, God "will lift [us] up." He will honor us. He will put us in a position of prominence in His Kingdom.

James thus ends where he began. "God opposes the proud, but gives grace to the humble." And we are responsible to take the steps that will result in humility, protecting us from Satan's efforts to cause us to stumble because of pride. In and of ourselves, of course, we cannot achieve these goals. But when we respond in obedience to the will of God, He will provide us with the inner strength and resources to "humble [ourselves] before God." If we don't respond in obedience, however, God will eventually humble us—not to punish us, but to discipline us and draw us close to Himself (see Heb. 12:4-11). Better to humble oneself as a Christian than to be humbled by God! It is far less painful!

AN OLD TESTAMENT SUMMARY

Psalm 1 summarizes James's concern more succinctly than any passage of Scripture I know. Read it carefully in view of what James has taught us and see if this is not true—

Blessed is the man
who does not walk in the counsel of the wicked
or stand in the way of sinners
or sit in the seat of mockers.
But his delight is in the law of the Lord,
and on his law he meditates day and night.
He is like a tree planted by streams of water,
which yields its fruit in season
and whose leaf does not wither.
Whatever he does prospers.

Not so the wicked!
They are like chaff
that the wind blows away.
Therefore the wicked will not stand in the judgment,
nor sinners in the assembly of the righteous.

For the Lord watches over the way of the righteous,
but the way of the wicked will perish.

A PERSONAL APPLICATION

Following is Psalm 1 paraphrased in the form of a personal prayer. Will you make this your prayer today?

> Father, help me not to walk in the counsel of the wicked, or to stand in the way of sinners or to sit in the seat of mockers. Help me to delight in your Word, to meditate on your truth at all times.
>
> Father, if I obey you in this way, I claim the promise that you will make me like a tree planted by streams of water, which yields its fruit in season and whose leaf does not wither. Thank you that you have promised that whatever I do will prosper.
>
> Father, may I never be like the wicked who are like chaff that the wind blows away. I am awed by the fact that the wicked will not stand in the judgment nor sinners in the assembly of the righteous and I grieve for those who follow the way of the wicked for they will perish.
>
> Father, I acknowledge that it is only by your grace that I am what I am and can be what you want me to be. Help me never to take pride even in the fact that you have chosen me. May I only fall at your feet and thank you for your marvelous love towards me.
>
> In the name of Jesus I pray. Amen.

7
THE SIN OF SLANDER
James 4:11-12

Brothers, do not slander one another. Anyone who speaks against his brother or judges him speaks against the law and judges it. When you judge the law, you are not keeping it, but sitting in judgment on it. There is only one Lawgiver and Judge, the one who is able to save and destroy. But you—who are you to judge your neighbor? (James 4:11-12)

In 1872 a group of men, including John Wesley, signed a covenant. Each agreed to hang it on the wall of his study. Following are the six articles in this solemn agreement:

1. That we will not listen or willingly inquire after ill concerning one another;
2. That, if we do hear any ill of each other, we will not be forward to believe it;
3. That, as soon as possible we will communicate what we hear by speaking or writing to the person concerned;
4. That, until we have done this, we will not write or

speak a syllable of it to any other person;

5. That neither will we mention it after we have done this, to any other person;
6. That we will not make any exception to any of these rules unless we think ourselves absolutely obliged in conference.

John Wesley and his friends provide an unusual example of God-fearing men who were determined to flesh out in their relationships with one another the spiritual lessons in James 4:11-12. After dealing with the "peril of pride," James wrote, "Brothers, do not slander one another" (4:11).

No message I've ever prepared has been more thought-provoking and in some respects, more personally convicting than this one. James's exhortation not to slander (literally "not to talk against") another Christian, brings every one of us face to face with our natural tendencies. Again and again I found myself evaluating my comments and statements—both past and present—in the light of this pointed exhortation. To be perfectly honest, I had to conclude that at times I most definitely have come up short in this area of my life when measured by God's standard.

On the other hand, I struggled with another question. When do statements of fact that seemingly must be said, actually become slander? After all, the Bible does not forbid a Christian from making statements about another Christian who is definitely out of the will of God. In fact, we are exhorted to admonish and confront one another. When making statements about another Christian that are negative, when do we step over the line and violate the will of God ourselves?

As I wrestled with my own personal shortcomings, as well as the issue of being appropriate when we do have to speak, I found myself engaging in a lot of personal introspection. To find answers I also sought guidance in other parts of Scripture to help me gain a broader perspective on this issue. I also interacted with other Christians regarding their opinions. What I'm about to share, therefore, has been put through three grids.

- My own personal experience and struggles in this area
- The insights and opinions of other Christians
- And most important, the teachings of Scripture.

A CONTEXTUAL PERSPECTIVE

To understand what James had in mind, it is helpful to look at the context leading up to this point in this letter. This is not the first time James warned against using the tongue in inappropriate ways. In fact, in each chapter preceding this exhortation in 4:11, he made some clear-cut statements regarding how a Christian should or should not communicate. If seen together, these statements provide a helpful profile for understanding James's overall concern regarding how we as Christians should or should not use our tongues. It also provides a context for understanding more closely this reference to the use of our tongue in 4:11.

Following are four pertinent statements from James's letter that establish this context, followed by a principle that emerges from each statement.

- *The exhortation:* 1:19-20, "My dear brothers, take note of this: Everyone should be quick to listen, slow to speak and slow to become angry, for man's anger does not bring about the righteous life that God desires."
- *The personal principle:* As a Christian I should always listen carefully and objectively and get as many facts as possible before I draw conclusions; furthermore, I should not speak out until I develop more objectivity by carefully thinking about what I've learned; and when I speak, it must not be motivated by quick-tempered anger that is

vindictive and causes me to take vengeance on another person.

• *The exhortation:* 2:12-13, "Speak and act as those who are going to be judged by the law that gives freedom, because judgment without mercy will be shown to anyone who has not been merciful. Mercy triumphs over judgment!"
• *The personal principle:* As a Christian I will be judged by God for the way I use my tongue. If I am not merciful, I will not be shown mercy. Practically speaking, this means I will be treated the way I treat others—even in this life. Critical people breed counter-criticism toward themselves.

Ultimately, however, Jesus taught that I will give an account for "every careless word" I speak (Matt. 12:36). In context, Jesus was definitely talking about communication that is motivated by sinful motives.

• *The exhortation:* 3:2, "We all stumble in many ways. If anyone is never at fault in what he says, he is a perfect man, able to keep his whole body in check."
• *The personal principle:* I will never be perfect in what I say. However, the degree to which I follow God's guidelines in what I say and the way I say it, reflects my level of spiritual maturity. Furthermore, it also determines the way I am able to control everything I do in relationship to God's will.

• *The exhortation:* 3:9, "With the tongue we praise our Lord and Father, and with it we curse men, who have been made in God's likeness. Out of the same mouth come praise and cursing. My brothers, this should not be."
• *The personal principle:* If I praise God with my words and at the same time I am hurting and tearing down other

Christians by what I say, I am in direct violation of the will of God.

A CLOSER LOOK

Let's now look at this passage in more detail. When James wrote, "Brothers, do not slander one another," he was definitely speaking in context. He does not want Christians to say things about other Christians that are destructive. Neither does he want us to hurt the work of God. Paul stated this truth positively when he wrote to the Ephesians, "Do not let any unwholesome talk come out of your mouth, but *only what is helpful for building others up according to their needs, that it may benefit those who listen* . . . . Get rid of all bitterness, rage and anger, brawling and slander, along with every form of malice," he continued. "Be kind and compassionate to one another, forgiving each other, just as in Christ God forgave you" (Eph. 4:29,31-32).

James proceeds to give four reasons in this paragraph why we should not "slander one another."

First, we are brothers and sisters in Christ. Three times in verse 11 alone James calls these people "brothers" (which includes sisters, since this is a generic term in the New Testament language). He wrote—"*Brothers,* do not slander one another. Anyone who speaks against his *brother* or judges *him* [literally 'his brother'] speaks against the law and judges it."

Throughout this whole letter, James continually reminded these Christians that they were "family." They were brothers and sisters. They belonged to each other and should be treating each other properly. Note that in six out of seven previous instances, when he used the word *brothers,* he was exhorting them to correct some problem in their relationship. The pattern is as follows:

- "Consider it pure joy, my *brothers,* whenever you face

trials of many kinds" (Jas. 1:2).

- "My *dear brothers,* take note of this: Everyone should be quick to listen, slow to speak and slow to become angry" (1:19).
- "My *brothers,* as believers in our glorious Lord Jesus Christ, don't show favoritism" (2:1).
- "Listen, my *dear brothers:* Has not God chosen those who are poor in the eyes of the world to be rich in faith and to inherit the kingdom he promised those who love him?" (2:5).
- "What good is it, my *brothers,* if a man claims to have faith but has no deeds?" (2:14).
- "Not many of you should presume to be teachers, my *brothers,* because you know that we who teach will be judged more strictly" (3:1).
- "Out of the same mouth come praise and cursing. My *brothers,* this should not be" (3:10).

And then, of course, in the passage in 4:11 he used the term *brothers* or *brother* three times in succession.

Why then should we treat one another properly as Christians—especially in what we say? It's because we are a family. We are to "be devoted to one another in *brotherly love*" (Rom. 12:10). We belong to each other. Paul admonished that we are to "do good to *all* people," but then he added—*"especially to those who belong to the family of believers"* (Gal. 6:10). In other words, Christians are not to slander anyone—even non-Christians. As Paul wrote to Titus, "Remind the people to be subject to rulers and authorities, to be obedient, to be ready to do whatever is good, *to slander no one,* to be peaceable and considerate, and to show true humility toward *all men*" (Titus 3:11-12). How tragic when we slander and speak against our own brothers and sisters in Christ!

Second, we are to be examples of love. The second reason Christians are not to slander one another is because it is in contradiction to everything that Jesus Christ taught and demonstrated. When we speak against a brother and sister in Christ, we are speaking "against the law."

Here James is probably referring to what he has identified earlier as the "royal law" of love which states: "Love your neighbor as yourself" (Jas. 2:8).

"To slander one another" is to walk deliberately out of the will of God. It is violating Christ's new commandment which He gave His followers when He said, "A *new commandment* I give you: *Love one another.* As I have loved you, so you must love one another" (John 13:34). And it is clear from Scripture that when we obey this commandment we are fulfilling the total law of God. It affects not only our relationship with God, but our relationship with all other people (see Rom. 13:8-10; Gal. 5:14).

Third, we are to submit to the Word of God. James makes it clear that when we slander a brother or sister in Christ, we're also slandering the Word of God and putting ourselves above the law. Thus James wrote, "Anyone who speaks against his brother or judges him speaks against the law and judges it. When you judge the law, you are not keeping it, but sitting in judgment on it" (Jas. 4:11).

To put it even more specifically, when we slander another Christian, we are deciding to pick and choose the area of God's Word that we want to obey. We put ourselves in the place of the divine "Lawgiver" and assume His authority. This is why James wrote that "there is only one Lawgiver and Judge, the one who is able to save and destroy" (Jas. 4:12). To judge is God's prerogative and His alone—not ours!

Paul elaborated on this point in his letter. We are not to "repay anyone evil for evil." We are not to "take revenge," but rather we are to "leave room for God's wrath, for it is written: 'It is mine to avenge; I will repay,' says the Lord." In this sense we are not to "be overcome by evil," rather we are to "overcome evil with good" (Rom. 12:17,19-21).

Fourth, we are to humble ourselves before God and others. To take the law of God in our own hands is the height of arrogance and pride. It is not an accident that James wrote about the sin of slander immediately following the section we've entitled the "peril of pride." Thus James wrote, "But you—who are you to judge your neighbor?" (Jas. 4:12b).

Pride, interwoven with feelings of insecurity, is often at the root of criticism towards others. We are "building ourselves up" by "tearing others down." Often we are trying to prove ourselves, and in so doing we are actually losing ground in destroying what credibility we have. In this sense, we are setting ourselves up for more rejection, further demotion, and continuing failure. We are facing the natural consequences of our critical spirit.

BIBLICAL BALANCE

James himself has given us some excellent guidelines to help us in being discreet in what we say to and about others. But there's much more in Scripture that gives us an even larger perspective on this subject, helping us to maintain proper balance, particularly when negative communication is unavoidable.

- *What if someone slanders me or sins against me in some specific way?*

If this is purely a personal matter, I should go to that person alone. If I get no results and feel it should be pursued, I can then take one or two other mature Christians with me. If there are still no results and it is a matter that should still be dealt with, I can take it to a larger group in the church. In the average church this should normally involve the spiritual leaders (see Matt. 18:15-17).

NOTE: There are some matters that should be dropped immediately if there is no response. To pursue the matter is often motivated by a desire to be vindicative. True, there may be times when this is necessary. But there are many instances where it is better to turn the problem over to the Lord and allow Him to deal with the situation. I have personally discovered that God is a great vindicator. His timing may not seem to coincide with mine, but when He deals with the problem, He does a much better job than I or anyone else could ever do.

- *What if the sin is openly committed against one or several Christians?*

If the sin becomes a public matter, it should be dealt with by several spiritual leaders in the church (see Gal. 6:1-3).

- *What should be our attitude when approaching another person about a personal or public offense?*

First, we should look carefully at our own lives. Jesus said, "Why do you look at the speck of sawdust in your brother's eye and pay no attention to the plank in your own eye? How can you say to your brother, 'Let me take the speck out of your eye,' when all the time there is a plank in your own eye? You hypocrite, first take the plank out of your own eye, and then you will see clearly to remove the speck from your brother's eye" (Matt. 7:3-5).

Second, we should have God's perspective on the matter. Paul wrote that we should be "complete in knowledge" in order to be able to admonish someone else (Rom. 15:14). In many instances we do not have all the facts either in the situation itself or in what God says about the matter. It is important that we have both.

Third, our goal should always be *restoration,* not condemnation (see Gal. 6:1).

Fourth, we should always approach these situations with a spirit of humility and gentleness (see Gal. 6:1-3; 2 Tim. 2:24-26). And we must always speak "the truth in love" (Eph. 4:15).

- ***What if a person does not respond to loving admonition and confrontation?***

If it is a matter involving more than a personal affront that cannot be overlooked and one which affects the Body of Christ and the work of God, the Scriptures clearly teach that a person should be disciplined under these circumstances. Both Jesus (Matt. 18:17) and Paul (Titus 3:10-11) made this clear. Paul told Titus: "Warn a divisive person once, and then warn him the second time. After that, have nothing to do with him. You may be sure that such a man is warped and sinful; he is self-condemned (Titus 3:10-11).

- ***What if the criticism is against a spiritual leader?***

Paul told Timothy not to receive "an accusation against an elder" (which would involve a spiritual leader generally) "unless it is brought by two or three witnesses" (1 Tim. 5:19). Obviously, to be qualified to bring this criticism, these individuals must meet the conditions already set forth. They themselves should have their lives in order before bringing accusations against a spiritual leader. Further, they must approach the situation with humility and a desire to restore; and they must always show respect and love.

- ***What if there are personality conflicts in a professional setting—for example, on the job?***

All of the foregoing guidelines should be considered in resolving this conflict as well. However, those who have managerial responsibilities in the organization are responsible to help solve these problems, since they involve the welfare of the total organization. We must respect lines of responsibility and authority.

A PERSONAL EXPERIENCE

Recently I was faced with a difficult problem that was far more than personal. It involved working with someone in another Christian organization. In order to achieve the goals of that organization, as well as the goals of the organization in which I'm involved, I was asked by a third party to look to this other person for assistance and help—which I was willing to do. However, I tried on several occasions to arrange communication with this other person, but to no avail. Frankly, I became very disturbed over the situation, feeling that I was being manipulated and put off. To make matters more complicated, I had personal dealings with this person previously that were rather painful—but I personally believe that I always handled the problem in a biblical way.

I found myself in a serious dilemma. How could I communicate with this third party who had asked me to submit myself to this individual without slandering or speaking against this other person?

First, I sought advice from my fellow pastors. Their initial recommendation was to wait and get perspective on the problem, since they sensed I was emotionally distraught over the situation.

Second, they suggested we pray that God would intervene in the situation and work in the hearts of everyone. Obviously, this was good advice. The more I waited, the more objectivity I developed, the more my anger subsided, and the more I solved my own wrong attitudes and actions in the situation.

To make a long story short, the Lord opened the door to talk to the third party in a sensitive, objective way—without having to speak against the brother I felt was manipulating me. I was able simply to present the facts in a nonpersonal way. The result was a miracle.

There are many details I could share to make this story more dramatic. But to share these details would be to violate the very principles in this chapter. Hopefully, the important lesson is clear, though the details are purposely withheld. I had to make sure my own heart was right, even though I felt that I was being unjustly treated in the situation. I needed to turn the matter over to the Lord for His help and guidance. And when I did, God helped me solve the problem without violating the principles of Scripture.

A PERSONAL CHALLENGE

How do you measure up to God's standards in your communication about others? Perhaps this poem will help you evaluate your life:

The Wrecking Crew

I stood on the street of a busy town
Watching men tearing a building down;
With a "ho, heave, ho," and a lusty yell
They swung a beam and a side wall fell.

I asked the foreman of the crew,
"Are those men as skilled as those you'd
Hire if you wanted to build?"
"Ah, no," he said, "no indeed,
Just common labor is all I need.

"I can tear down as much in a day or two
As would take skilled men a year to do."
And then I thought as I went my way,
Just which of these two roles am I trying to play?

Have I walked life's road with care
Measuring each deed with rule and square?
Or am I one of those who roam the town
Content with the labor of tearing down?

SOME CLOSING THOUGHTS

Will Rogers once said, "The only time people dislike gossip is when you gossip about them."

Someone has said, "It isn't the people who tell all they know that cause most of the trouble in this world; it's the ones who tell more."

Spurgeon once said, "Talebearing emits a three-fold poison; for it injures the teller, the hearer, and the person concerning whom the tale is told."

A four-year-old boy decided that he'd make an attempt at reciting the prayer he'd heard in church. "And forgive us our trashbaskets," he said, "as we forgive those who trashbasket against us."

8

THE UNCERTAINTY OF LIFE

James 4:13-17

Now listen, you who say, "Today or tomorrow we will go to this or that city, spend a year there, carry on business and make money." Why, you do not even know what will happen tomorrow. What is your life? You are a mist that appears for a little while and then vanishes. Instead, you ought to say, "If it is the Lord's will, we will live and do this or that." As it is, you boast and brag. All such boasting is evil. Anyone, then, who knows the good he ought to do and doesn't do it, sins. (James 4:13-17)

When Napoleon Bonaparte was planning to invade Russia, one of his influential advisors attempted to change his mind. Napoleon resisted his counsel. His advisor, not giving up, countered with the adage, "Sir," he said, "remember that man proposes, but God disposes."

Napoleon, enamored with his own sense of accomplishment, and captivated with pride and arrogance, would not listen. "I dispose as well as propose," he replied.

A Christian, overhearing the dialogue, predicted that this would be the turning point of this powerful leader's career. And it was! The invasion of Russia was the beginning of Napoleon's fall!

Many years earlier, another arrogant leader named Herod sat in his royal robes, delivering an address to the people in Tyre and Sidon. In order to ingratiate themselves with the king, the people responded, "This is the voice of a god, not of a man."

Herod's ego, which had already reached gigantic proportions, was inflated even more. He accepted the praise, and because he did, John records that "an angel of the Lord struck him down, and he was eaten by worms and died" (Acts 12:23).

Life is uncertain for all of us. True, men and women have been removed from this earth by the hand of God because of their pride and arrogance. It is dangerous to challenge God. But note also that before Herod was "struck down" by the Lord, he had taken the life of one of Christ's most trusted leaders—the Apostle James. Thousands of Christians over the years have faced martyrdom, not because of pride but because they have humbly submitted themselves to God and refused to deny His name. Being a Christian is no guarantee that we will have a long life on this earth.

The spiritual lesson James wanted his readers—and us—to learn from this next paragraph is that, because life is uncertain, we must live our lives with this in mind. Furthermore, we must use the time God gives us to serve God and others, doing all the good we can with our gifts, talents, abilities, and resources. His target audience is the Christian in business, but what he says applies to all believers in all circumstances.

A SOLEMN WARNING
(James 4:13-14a)

"Now listen, you who say, 'Today or tomorrow we will go to this or that city, spend a year there, carry on business and make money.' Why, you do not even know what will happen tomorrow."

No one knows the future—except God. True, the Lord has revealed a general outline concerning where history is going. We know that someday Jesus Christ will come and eternity will begin. It may be soon. Those who have accepted Jesus Christ as Saviour will spend eternity with God, and those who have rejected God's Son, will spend eternity separated from God.

But no one knows the details of the future, either for their own lives or for someone else's. On rare occasions God has periodically revealed some specific details through His gifted prophets, such as He did through Daniel (Dan. 5:26-28). But generally speaking, we do not know what tomorrow holds.

The call of death comes to every person, without exception, and has since the dawn of creation. Death often comes to people when it is not expected. A couple of years ago I took karate lessons from a young man by the name of Bob Lyle. Bob was a specimen of physical health. However, cancer struck! Within months God took him home.

Just a year ago a young woman was on her way to church—our church. Her car went out of control. Within seconds, she too was with the Lord. Her name was Laura and in our own church Media Center is a little plaque with a tribute to her life and ministry among us.

All of us can think of close friends and relatives who have seemed perfectly healthy one day and then suddenly their body is attacked by some serious disease. And there are those who die of heart attacks every day, some predictable and some totally without warning.

Why these illustrations? Because life is uncertain! James is correct. We do not know "what will happen tomorrow" (4:14).

Think for a moment. What if you had been on flight 007 headed for Seoul, Korea? I was on flight 372 headed for Buffalo, New York, when I was meditating on James's warning in these verses. I looked up from my Bible and glanced around the aircraft. Everything appeared normal. The flight was smooth, people were relaxed; some were reading, some were sleeping. A young couple was sitting in front of me with two small children. The little girl was snuggling up in her daddy's lap.

So it must have been that day on flight 007. Everything appeared normal. Some people were probably watching a movie, some reading a newspaper, some listening to stereophonic music or having a lighthearted conversation. Most were asleep. As on every commercial flight, businessmen or businesswomen, earlier during the flight, had no doubt been writing on yellow legal pads—working out a basic outline for a presentation. Some may have had calculators in hand, working on a special deal that would net their company a large sum of money and a personal commission that would provide financial security for perhaps years to come. James's warning is particularly applicable to them: "Now listen, you who say, 'Today or tomorrow we will go to this or that city [Seoul, or Tokyo, or Chicago—or Buffalo], spend a year there, carry on business and make money.' Why, you do not even know what will happen tomorrow."

No one on that Korean flight knew what was going to happen. No one, except the flight's cockpit crew, was even aware of the danger that lurked in the darkness. No passenger could hear the communications going on between the Russian pilots and their high command. Not until fiery rockets hit their plane did they know that death was imminent. And within moments—perhaps seconds—life on this earth was over for over 250 people.

A SIGNIFICANT QUESTION (James 4:14b)

After stating the uncertainty of life, James posed a question. "What is your life?" And then he used an illustration to answer that question. "You are a mist that appears for a little while and then vanishes."

When I left my hotel for the airport in Buffalo, New York, the whole city was covered with fog. But by the time I arrived at the terminal, it had lifted considerably and by the time we took off, it had almost disappeared. Within thirty minutes the mist had vanished. It was gone!

James is saying that life is like that mist! And even if we live a long life, it is but a moment on the continuum of history.

A STRAIGHTFORWARD EXHORTATION (James 4:15-17)

James first warned his readers regarding the uncertainty of life. He then told them why. Rather than making plans without God, they should always include God. Thus he wrote, "Instead, you ought to say, 'If it is the Lord's will, we live and do this or that'" (4:15).

These, of course, are not to be mere words we glibly utter and then go on our way, living our lives as if God did not exist. They should reflect a philosophy of life that affects *all* we say and do. It should be an attitude that is clearly visible in our actions.

How is this philosophy of life reflected? What is a true test that demonstrates that we are not merely giving verbal assent to what we know should be true? It is easy to say, "God willing." It is much more difficult to incorporate that truth into our work efforts. James gives us two ways to measure our perspective on life: through our humility and our unselfishness.

A Spirit of Humility (Jas. 4:16)

James illustrates this first characteristic with negative examples. He was writing to businessmen and women, some of whom claimed to be Christians but who operated on a purely humanistic level; in some respects they were no different from the atheist who actually denies that God exists. The only difference is that the atheist denies that God exists and lives with that viewpoint. On the other hand, the Christian business people, to whom James was writing, acknowledged God but lived *as if* He did not exist. That is why James wrote, "Now listen, you who say, 'Today or tomorrow we will go to this or that city, spend a year there, carry on business and make money'" (Jas. 4:13).

This is what they were saying—*and doing*! God had no place in their planning. They did not recognize Him as sovereign Lord of the universe and that without Him they could do nothing. Rather than reflecting the spirit of humility—which is *always* there if we truly recognize God's power and presence in the universe—they were boasting and bragging about their abilities, their opportunities, their business acumen. "All such boasting," James wrote, "is evil" (4:16).

One of the natural tendencies for every person, Christian and non-Christian, who lives in an environment where he can better himself, is to be lifted up with pride and take credit for his efforts to accumulate wealth. This is why God, through His servant Moses, warned the children of Israel against this tendency before He led them into the Promised Land. No doubt James had Moses' words in mind when he wrote this paragraph. Listen to what Moses said to Israel: "When you have eaten and are satisfied, praise the Lord your God for the good land he has given you. Be careful that you do not forget the Lord your God, failing to observe his commands, his laws and his decrees that I am giving you this day. Otherwise, when you eat and are satisfied, when you build fine houses and settle down, and when your herds and flocks grow large and your silver and gold increase and all you have is multiplied, then your heart will become proud and you will forget the Lord your God, who brought you out of Egypt, out of the land of slavery . . . . You may say to yourself, 'My power and the strength of my hands have produced this wealth for me.' But remember the Lord your God, for it is he who gives you the ability to produce wealth, and so confirms his covenant, which he swore to your forefathers, as it is today" (Deut. 8:10-14,17-18).

Unfortunately, Israel did not heed God's warning. They forgot the Lord. Their hearts were lifted up with pride. They took credit that belonged to God. And because they did, the Lord judged them as a nation and scattered them to the ends of the earth.

A true test, then, that we mean what we say *if* we say, "God willing," is that *all* we do is done in the spirit of humility. What successes we have will only serve to cause us to praise God and honor Him and thank Him for His leadership in our lives. We'll draw closer to Him and we'll not allow the good things God gives us to cause us to neglect our relationship with Him as well as our relationship with His people.

A Spirit of Unselfishness (James. 4:17)

The second test of whether or not we are truly putting God first in our lives is what we do with what God gives us. Thus James concludes this paragraph with this explicit exhortation, "Anyone, then, who knows the good he ought to do and doesn't do it, sins."

Here again, James is dealing with a natural tendency. There is within us all a desire to "carry on business and make money" (Jas. 4:13). And when this happens, our natural tendency is to want more and more and to keep more for ourselves. If this were not true, the Bible would not speak so frequently about the problem.

Remember the parable that Jesus told about the rich fool? Its message is clear. Listen: "The ground of a certain rich man produced a good crop. He thought to himself, 'What shall I do? I have no place to store my crops.' Then he said, 'This is what I'll do. I will tear down my barns and build bigger ones, and there I will store all my grain and my goods. And I'll say to myself, "You have plenty of good things laid up for many years. Take life easy; eat, drink and be merry."' But God said to him, 'You fool! This very night your life will be demanded from you. Then who will get what you have prepared for yourself?'" Jesus then made the application. It, too, is clear. Listen: "This is how it will be with anyone who stores up things for himself, but is not rich toward God" (Luke 12:16-21).

LESSONS IN PERSPECTIVE

What James Is Not Teaching

Before we state positively what James is teaching in this paragraph, it is necessary to make clear what he is *not* teaching.

First, he is not saying that we should be obsessed with the possibility of dying. True, life *is* uncertain. It *is* like "a mist that appears for a little while and then vanishes." But God does not want Christians to go through life worrying about the future. In this passage, James deals with reality. He did say, *"What is your life?"* But Jesus also said, *"Do not worry about your life"* (Matt. 6:25).

This is why a Christian has a unique advantage over

non-Christians. Life is uncertain for all of us! But a Christian knows that if life ceases here, it is just the beginning of a far better life. This is why Paul could write to the Philippians as he faced the possibility of execution, "For to me, to live is Christ and to die is gain" (Phil. 1:21).

I was very much impressed with the story of one of the passengers who boarded flight 007 in New York. Her name was Becky Scruton. Before she stepped on board, she shared with her friend who was with her that she planned to "share the Lord" with whoever might be sitting next to her. We're told that this kind of remark was very characteristic of Becky.

The year before, Becky's husband Dale died of cancer. As his pain grew ever more excruciating, Dale and Becky spent time praying together. Only minutes after his death, she stood in his hospital room and sang, "It Is Well with My Soul." Needless to say, every nurse in the room was moved to tears.

Becky's faith enabled her to handle the anxieties of raising their two children alone. As she put her energy into homemaking, she prayed for strength. But not even prayer and constant activity could keep the pain and loneliness at bay. She decided to go visit her parents in Seoul, Korea, where her father works as a civilian employee of the U.S. Army. She arranged to have her children stay with a friend and boarded flight 007. Little did she realize that, before the flight was over, she would join her husband in heaven.

But while she was on this earth, even as she boarded the flight, her priorities were straight. Her concern was that she might have an opportunity to share Jesus Christ with the person who sat beside her. Who knows? Perhaps there is someone in heaven today who would not be there if it had not been for Becky Scruton.

There is no way that we can completely understand

these events. For example, why would the Lord take the mother as well as the father and leave two children here? To try and answer that question would only throw us into a state of doubt and disillusionment. It's at times like this that we must trust God as the sovereign Lord of the universe. His ways are far beyond ours. But think what it would be like to face these possibilities without hope of eternal life! Though even life is uncertain, Jesus said, "Do not worry." Our lives are in His hands. We can trust Him.

Second, James is not teaching that we should not plan ahead. Neither is Jesus. It is not wrong to set financial goals. It is not wrong to "go to this city or that city" and conduct business. It is not wrong to spend "a year there," if necessary, to complete a transaction—provided we're not neglecting other biblical priorities in the process, such as our families. And it is not wrong to "make money."

Planning, therefore, is not wrong. In fact, Jesus made it clear that it is foolish *not* to plan. "Suppose," He said, "one of you wants to build a tower. Will he not first sit down and estimate the cost to see if he has enough money to complete it? For if he lays the foundation and is not able to finish it, everyone who sees it will ridicule him, saying, 'This fellow began to build and was not able to finish'" (Luke 14:28-30).

Third, James is not teaching that it is wrong to plan for our future security—particularly for our family. In fact, Paul states that a Christian is derelict if he doesn't care for his own family (1 Tim. 5:8). Many proverbs emphasize this same point.

What James Is Teaching

First, James was saying that in all of our planning, we must put God first. We must always "seek first his kingdom and his righteousness." Then, Jesus said, "All these things will be given you as well" (Matt. 6:33).

Second, James was teaching that we must live our lives on earth realizing that all we are and have come from Him. We have no right to take credit for our own accomplishments. The more God blesses, the more we should praise and thank Him.

Third, James was saying that when our accomplishments involve wealth, we should use it for the glory of God—not just simply to build a temporal kingdom. Perhaps no one is in a greater position to do more good than those who are in a position to make money.

It is true that God honors everything we do. The widow's mite is just as important to God as the rich man's millions. The talent we offer instead of cash is just as meaningful in God's sight. But the fact remains that money in large amounts enables God's work to go forward in unusual ways! It makes possible opportunities that otherwise would be impossible!

Let me share with you another unusual personal experience. As the primary leader of two growing organizations, Fellowship Bible Church North and the Center for Church Renewal, I realize every day how important money is in enabling these ministries to move forward. Any person who has an executive position in any organization can identify with my experience. The dynamics are the same. Money is the "bottom line" on the American business scene. Without it, a company cannot move forward. You can work and sweat and strive—but without capital you cannot succeed.

And so it is in God's work. Our goals, of course, are different. And as Christians, basic to all that we do must be prayer and faith. But the bottom line is still the same. We cannot pay salaries with verses and "prayer promises" from the Bible.

For some time one of my personal goals for the Center for Church Renewal was to be able to set up an internship program for men and women who are preparing for the ministry. In other words, we wanted to provide them with the opportunity to prepare for the ministry by being involved *in* the ministry. More specifically, we saw the possibility of selecting key seminary students who are already in training and provide them with supervised experience.

I shared this burden with the Center for Church Renewal and Fellowship Bible Church staff and together we've been praying about the possibility.

Several months ago, the Lord began to answer our prayers. He opened the door a crack when a Christian businessman in Dallas, who does not attend our church but who knows about our work, called and shared his burden which is very similar to ours. His interest was, of course, to provide financial assistance. This open door gave me an opportunity to share our burden regarding an internship program sponsored by the Center for Church Renewal and using Fellowship Bible Church North to gain experience under supervision.

To do this we would need to be able to provide these interns with financial assistance. In other words, rather than having them work at a secular job to provide for their personal needs, we would be able to remunerate them sufficiently so they would be able to spend their time ministering and learning at the same time.

In personal conversation with this gentleman, I shared with him that we could begin this program with at least six or seven interns. To finance the project we figured that it would take approximately $3,000 a month.

After listening to my proposal, he told me that he and his wife would definitely pray about being involved. Several weeks later I met at his home to discuss the project in more depth. As I was about to leave, he walked to his desk, opened his checkbook and wrote out a check and handed it to me. Frankly, I had not expected that immediate a response. When I looked at the check I could hardly believe my eyes. The amount was $36,000—the amount we would need to fund the internship program for a complete year.

I share this story for several reasons. For one thing, it was incredibly encouraging. I couldn't wait to share this answer to prayer with our staff—and especially with the prospective interns who I knew would be overjoyed with the opportunity.

I share it with you for a second reason. Without this kind of gift we would not be able to fund this internship program. The size of the gift definitely made a difference. Furthermore, it provided us with the security to know that we could do it for at least a year—something that would be very important to the interns themselves.

Thirdly, I saw in this man an incredible example of one who *is* making money—lots of it. But his primary concern is the kingdom of God. He has demonstrated that again and again. As he handed me the check, I looked into his eyes and said, "What can I say?" And as I stood there for that brief moment, I sensed a spirit of humility that was unusual in a moment like that. In fact, I saw what appeared to be tears of gratitude beginning to well up in his eyes, reflecting his thankfulness to God for being able to participate in this program.

Fourthly, he shared with me two things that ministered to me in a unique way. He made it clear that he wanted this money to be put to work immediately in the lives of these interns. In other words, he was saying this was for *this* year—not next year—to be used *now* for God's glory. He went on to explain that he wanted his money working for God immediately.

The second thing that he shared, which was very personal, was very encouraging. God now enabled him to give 50 percent of everything he makes to God's work. Here is a man who is truly giving as God is blessing.

What a contrast this is from the businessmen and women James is describing. But, this is the kind of men and women James wanted these people to become!

Thank God for those who are blessed with the gift of making money. But thank God that they do not allow it to control them, but continue to seek first the kingdom of God and His righteousness. Their ultimate goals are not temporal, but eternal!

9

THE WAGES OF WORLDLY WEALTH

James 5:1-6

Now listen, you rich people, weep and wail because of the misery that is coming upon you. Your wealth has rotted, and moths have eaten your clothes. Your gold and silver are corroded. Their corrosion will testify against you and eat your flesh like fire. You have hoarded wealth in the last days. Look! The wages you failed to pay the workmen who mowed your fields are crying out against you. The cries of the harvesters have reached the ears of the Lord Almighty. You have lived on earth in luxury and self-indulgence. You have fattened yourselves in the day of slaughter. You have condemned and murdered innocent men, who were not opposing you. (James 5:1-6)

One morning Elaine and I awakened early—part of the "old age" syndrome—and decided to go to our favorite place for fellowship—and food. The local donut shop! Usually there are several grandfatherly types sitting at the counter as early as four o'clock in the morning.

One of the men is named Earl. He is the most vocal,

and the loudest. He's losing his hearing. You can hear his resonant voice from one end of the place to the other.

On this particular morning he was telling the others how he had found a "wad of money" in a grocery store and decided to turn it in to the manager. All of the other old guys, almost in unison, pounced on him and in essence told him that he was nuts. Their continuing comments were interesting, to say the least.

"I'll tell you what they'll do," said one. "It will go into a 'baggers' money pool and everyone will get a piece of the action."

"Well, if it was $15," said one, "I'd have turned it in too. But if it was $15,000—well, I'd have probably kept it."

At that point they all laughed—including us. "See," one said, "we're all crooks. We just disagree on the amount."

"At least your conscience is clear, right, Earl?" said another. "Ya," said Earl—rather reluctantly (I think he was beginning to question his own sanity).

I leaned over to Elaine and told her, "There's my introduction to my next chapter in James."

Few people in this world would have done what Earl had done, particularly knowing that, in that situation, the manager would probably pocket the money—unless he was extremely benevolent and *did* decide to share it with the "baggers," his lowest paid employees. But unfortunately, few managers in this world would share this "windfall" with others. James spoke to that reality in the opening paragraph of chapter 5.

THE BIG PICTURE
(A Contextual Perspective)

To understand what James was saying, it is important to first of all look at the context—which quickly reveals he has changed audiences at this point in his letter. He was now speaking to those who were not Christians.

In the preceding paragraph (4:13-17) he was dealing with a similar subject: material wealth. However, he was speaking to believers, those who had put their faith in Jesus Christ for salvation. In essence he told them that when they went to "this or that city" and perhaps even spent "a year there" in order to "carry on business and make money," they should always do so with God in the center of their plans. Thus he said, "Instead [as a Christian], you ought to say, 'If it is the Lord's will, we will live and do this or that.'" God should always be at the center of our business activities. His honor and His glory should be uppermost in our minds and hearts because we don't know what the next day will bring forth. We should be aware every day of our lives that if it were not for God's grace and love, we could do nothing and achieve nothing in this world. This, of course, is true in the life of a non-Christian, whether that person realizes it or not. The Bible tells us that the sun shines and the rain falls on both the believer and the unbeliever (see Matt. 5:45). Without those two divine resources, no business could survive.

Another clue that James was speaking to non-Christians in this paragraph is the obvious omission of the word *brothers*. Just *before* he transitioned into the paragraph, emphasizing that Christians should consider God in their plans to make money, James used the word *brothers* or *brother* two times in one verse (Jas. 4:11). And *following* the paragraph directed at non-Christians, which we'll look at in this chapter, he again used the word *brothers*—four times to be exact. It is obvious he was going back to his original audience—believers. Note the following statements:

- "Be patient, then, *brothers,* until the Lord's coming" (Jas. 5:7).

- "Don't grumble against each other, *brothers,* or you will be judged" (5:9).
- "*Brothers,* as an example of patience in the face of suffering, take the prophets who spoke in the name of the Lord" (5:10).
- "Above all, my *brothers,* do not swear—not by heaven or by earth or by anything else" (5:12).

THE BACKDROP
(An Historical Perspective)

There is a perspective in James's mind that goes beyond the immediate context in this letter. He is speaking both historically and prophetically. The prophetic perspective involves the words of Jesus to the people living in Jerusalem before His crucifixion. "The days will come upon you," He said, "when your enemies will build an embankment against you and encircle you and hem you in on every side. They will dash you to the ground, you and the children within your walls. They will not leave one stone on another, because you did not recognize the time of God's coming to you" (Luke 19:43-44).

We're not exactly sure when James wrote his letter. But we know, of course, it was before Jesus' prophecy was fulfilled regarding Jerusalem in A.D. 70. What James (and Jesus) said would happen, happened! The Roman army, led by Titus, beseiged Jerusalem. They surrounded the city and, 143 days later, the city fell. The final fall probably came during the hottest time of the year, which intensified the suffering from disease, famine, and thirst. So complete was the devastation that Jerusalem had no history for sixty years. Everything Jesus said literally came true.

A great number of the unsaved Jews whom James was addressing in this paragraph lived in Jerusalem. Thus he warned them, "Now listen, you rich people, weep and wail because of the misery that is coming upon you. Your wealth has rotted, and moths have eaten your clothes. Your gold and silver are corroded" (Jas. 5:1-3a).

Many rich and wealthy Jews who had rejected their Messiah and instead had put their hope in riches lost it all when Titus and his Roman legions destroyed Jerusalem. The bloody seige claimed over a million lives. Thus Jesus' prophecy (and James's) was literally fulfilled. But there is much more in these verses than the historical perspective. Let's look more carefully at what James wrote.

A CLOSEUP
(A Textual Perspective)

The Temporariness of Worldly Wealth (James 5:1-3a)

The first point James made is that material things do not provide ultimate happiness. A person can be wealthy and miserable even in this life. It is no substitute for the spiritual aspects of life. John D. Rockefeller, Jr., once said that "the poorest man I know is the man who has *nothing* but money." And Andrew Carnegie, a multi-millionaire said, "Millionaires seldom smile." These men are simply verifying what James wrote when he warned unsaved rich people to "weep and wail because of the misery" that is coming upon them (Jas. 5:1).

Secondly, James was saying that material things are not enduring. They "rot." Even our finest clothes deteriorate. And James says that "gold and silver" will corrode, or more literally "rust." This is a very striking statement since "gold and silver" do not literally rust (see 5:2-3).

Is this a contradiction? Not at all! James was simply making the point that even "gold and silver"—which are the most enduring metals—will ultimately disappear and become meaningless. Of course, when we die we leave it all behind. We cannot take it with us. In eternity we will have nothing—unless we know Jesus Christ and, as Christians, have used our wealth to build God's eternal kingdom.

The Tragedy of Worldly Wealth (James 5:3b)

What happens when a man or woman puts his or her confidence in gold or silver and other material things for security, rather than in Jesus Christ? In true "James fashion," he spoke to this question clearly, succinctly, and forthrightly. "Their corrosion will testify against you," he wrote, "and eat your flesh like fire" (Jas. 5:3b).

While Jesus was on earth, He told a dramatic story that helps us understand what James had in mind with this statement. "There was a rich man," Jesus said, "who was dressed in purple and fine linen and lived in luxury every day. At his gate was laid a beggar named Lazarus, covered with sores and longing to eat what fell from the rich man's table." Eventually this poor beggar died and joined his father Abraham in heaven. Later, this wealthy man Jesus used in His illustration also faced death. However, he did not go to join his father Abraham. Rather, Jesus stated, "In hell, where he was in torment, he looked up and saw Abraham far away, with Lazarus by his side."

The rich man called out to Abraham for pity and asked that Lazarus, the poor beggar who had lain at his gate, be sent "to dip the tip of his finger in water and cool" the rich man's tongue. "I am in agony in this fire," the rich man said.

Abraham's response to the rich man's request is sobering. "Son, remember that in your lifetime you received your good things," Abraham replied, "while Lazarus received bad things, but now he is comforted here and you are in agony."

Accepting the fact that nothing could be done for himself, the rich man made another request. He asked that Lazarus be sent to warn his five brothers who were living the same life-style as he had lived. And again, Abraham's response is sobering. "They have Moses and the Prophets; let them listen to them," responded Abraham.

The rich man tried again and begged Abraham to send Lazarus, because if Lazarus came back from the dead, the man was sure his brothers would repent.

Once again, Abraham responded with bad news. "If they do not listen to Moses and the Prophets, they will not be convinced even if someone rises from the dead" (Luke 16:19-31).

With this story Jesus was illustrating in detail what James was saying in one succinct statement: The rich man's gold and silver and his fine linen clothes were corroded and that corrosion was testifying against him and eating his "flesh like fire."

James was saying something else that correlates with the major truth Jesus was communicating with His parable. Someone *had* risen from the dead! He was the Messiah. He walked among these Jews. He demonstrated His deity in many ways, but in no way more specifically and dramatically than through the Resurrection. Yet these rich Jews had rejected Jesus Christ and had put their hope in their material possessions. This explains why James wrote with a sense of finality regarding the judgment that was coming upon them. The rich Jews had hardened their hearts against God and sealed their destiny. Like the rich man's five brothers who appear in Jesus' story, they would not listen even to someone who had come back from the dead. And indeed, the rich Jews whom James was writing to had proved that very point!

Eternal separation from God is a certainty! "Fire" is often used in Scripture to illustrate the environment.

Other passages refer to everlasting "darkness" and "aloneness." Just what form hell will take is subject to discussion. But whatever it is like, it will be a place of torment and lostness forever. And the Bible clearly teaches that people who do not know Christ personally are doomed to spend eternity there, separated from God. And as Jesus illustrated, there will be "a great chasm" between those who are lost and those who are saved. It will be impossible to cross over that chasm (Luke 16:26)!

The Temptations of Worldly Wealth (James 5:3c-6)

As James described the behavior of these rich people in the remaining sentences in this paragraph, he was outlining in a functional way the temptations faced by wealthy people, particularly those who are not true Christians.

To accumulate more and more (Jas. 5:3c): "You have hoarded wealth in the last days," James stated. In other words, he was saying these rich people had accumulated more and more. They never had enough to satisfy them. They were perfect examples of the rich fool Jesus described in His story recorded in Luke's Gospel. This man's crops had multiplied to the place where he had no more room. Though he built barns, in his heart he was saying to himself, "You have plenty of good things laid up for many years. Take life easy; eat, drink and be merry" (Luke 12:19).

Unfortunately, that very night this man's life was taken. And, of course, he left it all behind. And the implication is that he faced eternity without God.

To be unfair and dishonest (Jas. 5:4): Not only did these rich people accumulate more and more for themselves, but they actually "failed to pay the workmen" they had hired to take care of their fields. They were not fair. They were unethical and dishonest. And James went on to say that "the cries of the harvesters" who had been cheated had "reached the ears of the Lord Almighty" (Jas. 5:4).

It is sad but true. Those who put their confidence in wealth rather than in Christ are frequently selfish and dishonest. They take advantage of the poor in their own society. This is why the American government, for example, has had to establish labor laws and minimum wage standards. If they had not, people with money would take advantage of people who don't have it. It is a sad commentary on a nation that claims to be Christian in its basic values.

James made it clear that God will not tolerate this kind of behavior. There will come a day of reckoning. Thus he said, "The cries of the harvesters have reached the ears of the Lord Almighty" (5:4b).

To be self-indulgent (Jas. 5:5): James accused these rich people of having "lived on earth in luxury and self-indulgence."

This should not surprise us! When our security is in material things, we attempt to satisfy ourselves with more things. But when we do, wrote James, we have "fattened ourselves" in the "day of slaughter." We are only preparing ourselves for a tragic end.

We have often heard about the group of men who were considered the most successful financiers, who met in Chicago at the Edgewater Beach Hotel in 1923. In fact, I mentioned them in volume 1 in our study of James. But their story bears repeating.

Collectively, these tycoons controlled more wealth than there was in the United States treasury, and for years newspapers and magazines had been printing their success stories and urging the youth of the nation to follow their examples.

Twenty-seven years following this meeting, here is what had happened to each of these men.

- Charles Schwab, the president of the largest steel company, lived on borrowed money the last five years of his life and died penniless.
- Arthur Cutten, the greatest wheat speculator, died abroad insolvent.
- Richard Whitney, the president of the New York Stock Exchange, spent time in Sing Sing prison.
- Albert Fall, the member of the President's cabinet, was pardoned from prison so he could die at home.
- Jesse Livermore, the greatest bear on Wall Street, committed suicide.
- Leon Fraser, the president of the Bank of International Settlement, also committed suicide.
- Ivar Krueger, the head of the world's greatest monopoly, also committed suicide.

All of these men had learned how to make money, but not one of them had learned how to live. Indeed, James was right when he said, "You have fattened yourselves in the day of slaughter."

To be unethical and immoral (Jas. 5:6): James concluded this paragraph with his severest criticism. He wrote, "You have condemned and murdered innocent men, who were not opposing you" (5:6).

It is tragic that the temptation to accumulate wealth leads people to engage in behavior that is beyond belief. How many times do stories regarding money-related homicides appear in our daily newspapers? True, there are those who rob and kill because they do not have money, but many times murders take place in exclusive surroundings—a battle between those who are rich and who want more.

It is even more tragic when rich people trample over innocent people in order to become richer. Unfortunately, money talks—even in our courts of law.

And so James lowered the boom on those who are rich

in this world but who had turned away from God and rejected the Lord Jesus Christ. They were not merely *headed* for serious trouble—they were *already in* serious trouble! In God's mind their wealth had already rotted and their clothes were already eaten by moths. Their gold and silver were corroded. Though everything looked all right to the casual observer, these rich were only one step away from the most tragic thing that can happen to any individual—eternal separation from God!

A MESSAGE TO YOU AND ME

The temptation for any Christian hearing these words from James is to conclude that there is really nothing in this section for believers. After all, James *was* directing his statements to the unsaved. However, we must remember that "not all Scripture is written *to us,* but all Scripture is written *for us*"—to quote John Blanchard.[1] There is a message for every Christian in this passage.

First, let it be said again that James was not condemning the man or woman—Christian or non-Christian—who is wealthy. Money, per se, is not evil. That is not the issue in this passage. As we've seen from the previous paragraph (see chapter 8), James was concerned that Christians who are in the business of making money should always put God in the center of that process. And in this paragraph, directed to unbelievers, he is saying that money should not be a substitute for God. When we leave God out of the process completely, we will experience unhappiness now and eternally.

But what *is* James saying specifically to Christians? Experience verifies that Christians are not exempt from the very temptations that non-Christians face—particularly when we have opportunity to accumulate material things.

- If we're not on guard against Satan, the more we get the

more we want! We become obsessed with accumulating things.

- If we're not on guard against Satan, we'll be tempted to be unfair and dishonest in the process of accumulating wealth.
- If we're not on guard against Satan, we'll be tempted to become self-indulgent.

NOTE: There's a fine line here. In some respects, the amount of wealth a person has and how that person lives is relative. We must be careful that we do not judge one another in these matters. However, every Christian must judge himself. He must constantly ask himself the question—if he has excess money—am I being self-indulgent? This question must be answered against the backdrop of our commitment to Jesus Christ and how we use what we have to honor and glorify our Lord.

- If we're not on guard against Satan, we may get caught up in unethical and even immoral behavior. We may not kill someone because of covetousness, but there are some who end up, for example, destroying other people's marriages. Furthermore, on occasions, this process has resulted in suicide. One wonders how James would evaluate this kind of situation. Is it not murder?

But let me get even more personal. Many of the people I minister to live in North Dallas. And even more specifically, many live in Plano, Texas—a North Dallas suburb that has made national headlines because of teenage suicides. It was reported in the *Dallas Morning News* "that not everyone agrees on why Plano's teenage suicide rate" in 1983 was "almost ten times the national average."

Debra Martime went on to outline some of the reasons Plano people gave for these suicides. "Some blame Plano's boom town personality," she wrote. "Others say that the last five victims were 'copycats,' and that the idea was planted in their minds by news reports. Still others say

Plano's loose-knit success-oriented family life contributed to the deaths. And there are those who discount all of these reasons. They say the suicides are all isolated incidents and they say what has happened in Plano can happen anywhere."

Martime, the author of this report, was not satisfied, however, with the ambiguity of these reasons. She went on to point out that what "happened in Plano hasn't happened just anywhere." To make her point she outlined these interesting facts:

- From 1970 to 1980, Plano's population grew 300 percent at a time when the national growth rate was 11.4 percent.
- Plano has become well known for being affluent, educated, and white collar. The average Plano family earns a third more money than the average American family.
- One out of three Plano residents has completed four or more years of college, whereas, nationally, fewer than one out of five Americans has completed four or more years of college.
- About 80 percent of the Plano labor force are white-collar workers, whereas nationally the figure is about 53 percent.

Perhaps one of the most astute observations is that Plano shares these above-average qualities with other American communities:

- Malibu and San Mateo, California
- West Palm Beach, Florida
- The Denver suburb of Cherry Creek
- Morris County, New Jersey
- The Chicago suburbs along Lake Michigan's North Shore.

Significantly, every one of these areas has experienced a number of adolescent suicides disproportionate to the national rate.

Those who have studied affluent communities point out several conditions that exist in these areas which have contributed to higher teen suicides.

1. Parents tend to treat their children as "status symbols."
2. Parents often pressure their children to be overachievers.
3. Parents tend to shelter their children from decision-making.
4. Teenagers themselves develop social structures that encourage exclusive cliques.
5. Since these communities are so new, residents find it difficult to develop a sense of belonging.

What does all of this say to those of us who are Christians? And, of course, what could be said about Plano, Texas, could be said about many more American cities.

Even though Martime's analysis may be incorrect in certain particulars, it says we must take James's teachings seriously. Affluence can be a blessing or a curse. As Christian parents we must make sure that we put Jesus Christ first in our total life-style. We must not succumb to the temptations that *always* accompany affluence. If we do, we may pay a terrible price—hopefully not losing a family member in the tragic way others have experienced; but it will inevitably show up in other ways.

A POSITIVE PERSPECTIVE

- Let us thank God for our blessings.
- Let us thank God that we have opportunities to better ourselves.
- Let us thank God we have many wonderful conveniences.
- Let us thank God for the enjoyment we can experience with these blessings.

A WORD OF CAUTION

Let us pray that we will not become materialistic. Let us pray for wisdom to rear our children wisely—not withholding things per se to teach them spirituality, for that will only create a desire for things. But neither must we provide them with so much that they grow up leaving God out of their lives.

A FINAL NOTE

The greatest way to achieve spirituality in our children is to be spiritual examples ourselves. Therefore, we must face and answer a very practical question: Am I an example of being spiritual, or am I an example of being materialistic? Every believer is responsible to answer that question in the light of the principles of Scripture. Furthermore, we must not put off facing that question. It is one that we *must* face and answer *now* and in the days that lie ahead.

A PROMISE FROM JAMES

"If any of you lacks wisdom, he should ask God, who gives generously to all without finding fault, and it will be given to him" (Jas. 1:5).

Note

1. John Blanchard, *Not Hearers Only,* vol. 4 (London: Word Books, 1974), p. 12.

10

PATIENCE AND PERSEVERANCE IN PAIN

James 5:7-12

Be patient, then, brothers, until the Lord's coming. See how the farmer waits for the land to yield its valuable crop and how patient he is for the autumn and spring rains. You too, be patient and stand firm, because the Lord's coming is near. Don't grumble against each other, brothers, or you will be judged. The Judge is standing at the door!

Brothers, as an example of patience in the face of suffering, take the prophets who spoke in the name of the Lord. As you know, we consider blessed those who have persevered. You have heard of Job's perseverance and have seen what the Lord finally brought about. The Lord is full of compassion and mercy.

Above all, my brothers, do not swear—not by heaven or by earth or by anything else. Let your "Yes" be yes, and your "No," no, or you will be condemned. (James 5:7-12)

The story is told of Hachi, a Japanese dog, that would accompany his master to the railroad station every morning. And every evening Hachi would be back to greet his friend, tail wagging, as his master arrived home from work.

One night, however, the dog's master did not return. He had traveled to another city that day and while there, died. Hachi, unable to comprehend the situation, continued to go to the railroad station every evening, and faithfully and patiently waited for at least an hour for his master's return. He then turned and sadly trotted home. This he did every evening—for over ten years.

Hachi's faithfulness so impressed the Japanese people that the government erected a statue of the dog on the spot where he had so patiently waited—and then sent statuettes to all the schools in what was then the Japanese Empire.

Isn't it interesting that animals sometimes demonstrate a quality of loyalty, patience, and perseverance unknown to the world of human beings. True, Hachi's intelligence was limited. No one could explain to him that his master would never return.

But, again, the contrast is startling! As Christians we *do* understand that our Master will someday return. And yet we have difficulty demonstrating, as we would like and should, the qualities of patience and faithfulness and perseverance. James next spoke to this human weakness in us all.

James's concerns in verses 7 to 12 can be summarized with two basic exhortations:

- "*Be patient,* then, brothers until the Lord's coming" (Jas. 5:7a).
- "*Stand firm,* because the Lord's coming is near (Jas. 5:8b).

"BE PATIENT"
(James 5:7)

The Audience

Note first that James once again was directing his thoughts to Christians. Four times within the span of six verses he used the word "brothers." For a brief moment he had directed some very strong statements at those who were rich in this world, but not rich in Christ. They were unbelievers.

The Continuity

Note, secondly, the continuity between what he had just said to those without Christ and what he is now saying to believers. It was the non-Christians who had been mistreating the Christians. While they built their financial kingdoms they had not paid their employees the wages they deserved. Evidently, a number of believers were among those who had received this ill treatment.

To make matters worse, these unbelieving kingdom-builders were living in luxury and self-indulgence while those who worked for them did not have enough income to take care of their own personal needs.

It also appears that some of these believers were being falsely accused and even sentenced to death, based on trumped-up charges against them. Their wealthy employers had evidently used their financial power to bring judgments against them even though they were innocent of any wrongdoing.

It was in this context that James encouraged these New Testament Christians to "be patient . . . [until] the Lord's coming."

A Definition

The word James used which is translated "patient" actually refers to being "longsuffering." He was encouraging these Christians not to retaliate with resentment and anger, but to patiently endure this mistreatment, realizing that someday Jesus Christ would deliver them from their pain and suffering.

We must realize there was very little these believers could do to protect themselves. In their culture they had no channels as we do to guarantee personal rights. To fight back would only agitate their employers and intensify the persecution. Thus, their hope in Christ—particularly to be delivered from this evil world at His second coming—became very meaningful to them.

An Illustration

To get his point across, James used an illustration. He referred to the farmer who "waits for the land to yield its valuable crop." He called attention to the farmer's patience after he once sowed the seed and waited "for the autumn and spring rains" (Jas. 5:7b). Just so, James says, "You too, be patient" (5:8).

Having been reared on a farm in Indiana, I can certainly identify with this illustration. I remember the times when we planted corn and then waited for rain. There were times when it didn't come and the seed lay in the ground, unable to germinate because of the lack of moisture. There were also times when there was enough moisture to cause the seeds to sprout and begin to grow, but lack of further rain caused the plants to stop growing. Leaves turned yellow and then brown. And I remember times when there was not enough moisture for the ears of corn to develop on the stalks.

Those days of waiting were trying and difficult for my father, because a bad crop would mean a poor harvest. And a poor harvest meant little or no income for that year. And all of us can identify to some degree with what it means to lose a year's income, especially when you've used all your reserves to prepare the soil, buy the seed and fertilizer, and to go to the effort of planting the fields.

It would do no good, of course, to attack the fields, to vent our wrath on the withering stalks of corn, or to shake our fists at God. For the Christian—and my dad was a Christian—it meant patiently trusting God no matter what the circumstances. And though there were some tense and difficult periods of time over the years, the Lord never failed us. I never remember ever having missed a meal. I always had clothes to wear and a place to live in security and safety.

Thus, James encouraged these Christians to face their trying circumstances with patience and longsuffering—just as a farmer patiently waits for the rain to fall and for his land to produce crops. They were not to attack their persecutors, for that would only make the problem worse. They were not to take matters into their own hands, for if they did, they would only intensify their persecution and bring more suffering.

Their immediate hope was to respond patiently, hoping that their good behavior would bring compassion from their tormentors. And their ultimate hope was that someday Jesus Christ would come and deliver them from their painful circumstances.

"STAND FIRM" (James 5:8-9)

In verse 8, James adds a second dimension to his first exhortation. They were not only to "be patient," but to "stand firm." Once again James's appeal was based on the hope that Christ would soon come to deliver them (Jas. 5:8).

A Definition

To "stand firm" means to "establish their hearts" in

the midst of their trials and in full light of what may happen. Here James used the same basic word Luke used to describe Christ's attitudes and actions when He headed for Jerusalem, knowing what awaited Him there. Luke recorded, "As the time approached for him to be taken up to heaven, *Jesus resolutely set out for Jerusalem*" (Luke 9:51). The King James reads, "And it came to pass, when the time was come that he should be received up, he *stedfastly set his face* to go to Jerusalem."

John Blanchard, in his commentary on James, captures the essence of what James was communicating when he wrote: "The Bible does not speak of patience in terms of waiting for something to happen, but rather a steadfast endurance while things *are* happening, and of pressing on regardless of what *will* happen."[1]

A Practical Problem

James deals next with a very practical problem that always emerges in times of difficulty. When the pressure is on, particularly from outside sources, and when there is little that can be done to alleviate the problem, there's a tendency to become short-tempered and impatient with those close to you. No doubt this was happening among the Christians James was writing to. Thus, he exhorted them, "Don't grumble against each other, brothers, or you will be judged. The Judge is standing at the door!" (Jas. 5:9).

Have you ever experienced this phenomenon in your own life? What happens when you're under pressure, when you're frustrated and particularly when you seemingly can't do anything about it? If you're like I am, those closest to me are the ones who feel the fallout from my resentment; namely, my wife and children. It's at times like these that we tend to displace our hostility and, ironically, those we care about the most catch the full weight of our anger.

And so it is with the family of God. The believers James is writing to were facing severe trials. They were being mistreated. To defend themselves would mean even greater mistreatment. Consequently, they began to "grumble against each other"—to displace their hostility on those within the church.

James warned them to avoid such behavior, because the very One who would come someday to deliver them from their problems would have to judge them for being impatient with one another during their problems.

BIBLICAL EXAMPLES (James 5:10-12)

To encourage these Christians, James next drew on biblical history—examples of men and women who also suffered and yet endured the pain with patience. Thus he wrote, "Brothers, as an example of patience in the face of suffering, take the prophets who spoke in the name of the Lord. As you know, we consider blessed those who have persevered. You have heard of Job's perseverance and have seen what the Lord finally brought about. The Lord is full of compassion and mercy" (5:10-11).

With the exception of Job, James simply generalized and referred to "the prophets who spoke in the name of the Lord." Being Jewish Christians, these people would immediately identify a number of these Old Testament personalities.

The Hebrew Hall of Faith

There's another letter in the New Testament, however, which was also written to Jewish Christians, and which expands this generalization with numerous examples. The letter is the Epistle to the Hebrews. And chapter 11 is often called the "Old Testament Hall of Faith." In this chapter the author (some think it was Paul, but we really don't know for sure) referred to Abel, Enoch, Noah, Abraham, Isaac, Jacob, Joseph, Moses, and even the prostitute Rahab, whose life was dramatically changed through an encounter with the living God.

"And what more shall I say?" we read in verse 32. "I do not have time to tell about Gideon, Barak, Samson, Jephthah, David, Samuel and the prophets, who through faith conquered kingdoms, administered justice, and gained what was promised; who shut the mouths of lions, quenched the fury of the flames, and escaped the edge of the sword; whose weakness was turned to strength; and who became powerful in battle and routed foreign armies. Women received back their dead, raised to life again. Others were tortured and refused to be released, so that they might gain a better resurrection. Some faced jeers and flogging, while still others were chained and put in prison. They were stoned; they were sawed in two; they were put to death by the sword. They went about in sheepskins and goatskins, destitute, persecuted and mistreated—the world was not worthy of them. They wandered in deserts and mountains, and in caves and holes in the ground" (Heb. 11:32-38).

The author of this Hebrew letter culminates this letter with a very interesting observation: "These were all commended for their faith, yet none of them received what had been promised. God had planned something better for us so that only together with us would they be made perfect" (11:39-40).

But even more significant, the author moves on to apply the lessons we can learn from these Old Testament greats. And what he says in the opening part of chapter 12 is a beautiful compliment to what James was saying in the paragraph before us. "Therefore," he wrote, "since we are surrounded by such a great cloud of witnesses, let us throw off everything that hinders and the sin that so easily entangles, and let us run with perseverance the race marked out for us. Let us fix our eyes on Jesus, the author and perfector of our faith, who for the joy set before him endured the cross, scorning its shame, and sat down at the right hand of the throne of God" (12:1-2).

James did become specific in his reference to Job, a well-known Old Testament personality. He lost everything—his children, his wealth, his friends. What's more, his physical suffering was beyond human comprehension. His body was covered with painful boils. Even his wife told him to curse God and die.

Though Job wavered, though he questioned God, though he became disoriented and confused, he never turned against God. And in the end, God blessed him far beyond anything he'd ever experienced before. You see, James was saying, "The Lord *is* full of compassion and mercy" (Jas. 5:11). We may not understand His timetable or our particular circumstances, but God *does* love and care for us. And even when we create our own problems, He is ready and willing to meet our needs.

Some Final Exhortations

Interestingly, some Christians who become the most impatient with God and others are those who have created the problems in the first place. It is unfortunate, indeed, when we blame others for our own mistakes. It is the ultimate in insensitivity and selfishness. Perhaps this is one of the reasons James had to also say, "Don't grumble against each other, brothers, or you will be judged" (Jas. 5:9).

James ends this paragraph with an exhortation that is difficult for us to understand. One thing is extremely clear, however. It was a very important concern, for James wrote, "*Above all,* my brothers, do not swear—not by heaven or by earth or by anything else. Let your 'Yes' be yes, and your 'No,' no, or you will be condemned" (5:12).

To understand what James meant we must understand first what he didn't mean. He was not referring to "swearing" in the sense of taking the name of the Lord in vain. Certainly, we should not violate this commandment. But this is not what James had in mind. And he certainly was not saying it is wrong for a Christian to take an oath today in a court of law. For a Christian, of course, that oath should not be necessary because we should always be committed to telling the truth and nothing but the truth. Thus a Christian should not hesitate to take that kind of oath, for he is committed to being honest in the first place.

What then was James saying? Confirming something by an oath was very common in both Old Testament and New Testament history. But the process had fallen into disrepute because it was abused and misused. Oath-taking became a sham and simply a meaningless routine. In actuality, what was to be a means to guarantee honesty became a way to be dishonest by outwardly attempting to demonstrate "honesty" and, at the same time, to proceed to be dishonest.

Thus we can see James's concern. In the midst of persecution and trials, he was encouraging these Christians to be straightforward and honest. They were to just say "yes" when they meant yes and "no" when they meant no. To attempt to straddle the fence would only lead them into deeper trouble. Not only would they be judged by the Lord for being dishonest, but they would ultimately intensify their problems in relating to both Christians and non-Christians. It is one thing to follow the Lord's instruction and be as wise as a serpent and as harmless as a dove. It is another to be political, dishonest, and manipulative. That kind of behavior ultimately backfires and does more harm than good. In essence, James was saying be straightforward and honest—and trust the results to God.

THE TWENTIETH-CENTURY CHRISTIAN

How do we, in the twentieth century, handle patience, perseverance and pain? In some respects it is difficult to hurdle the two-thousand-year chasm that exists between us and those who lived in the first century. There is very little circumstantial relationship between the world most of us know and the world most New Testament Christians experienced. Persecution was often rampant—particularly for the Jewish Christians James was writing to. He was really ending this letter where he began when he wrote, "Consider it pure joy, my brothers, whenever you face trials of many kinds" (Jas. 1:2). Life was unusually difficult for those believers.

On the other hand, throughout Church history, Christians at various times and in various places have faced severe persecution. Sometimes it has been directed at them specifically and many have lost their lives. At other times they have simply been victims of the general unrest that existed in their society.

For example, I was listening to a radio interview with a pastor in El Salvador, Central America, the very week I was writing this chapter. For a period of time, Christians were victims of the war that existed in that country. He told about the fact that during a two-year period, over two hundred people were killed within a block of his own home. He told of having to end several church services where the people were on the floor with bullets flying over their heads. One member of the church was actually assassinated coming into the church building. On one occasion a McDonald's restaurant, located a block from the church, was blown up. This pastor also told about the students who attended the seminary they conducted in their church. During this period of unusual unrest, these students actually risked their lives every evening to attend classes.

For those of us who have never experienced this type of difficulty, it is always amazing to see how Christians respond. Life goes on—victoriously. In this situation in El Salvador, the church continued to grow and thrive, as it usually does in times of trial and persecution. In fact, Christianity becomes much more real. Theological concepts like "trust" and "faith" and "prayer" take on an entirely new meaning. The glorious truth of the second coming of Christ becomes especially meaningful.

Let's remember that there are Christians in the world today who face incredible persecution. James's words in this passage would be very meaningful and encouraging to them since they would literally identify with the circumstances.

But let's remember also that problems and the pain they create are relative. It is possible to be free from persecution and danger and yet be in deep emotional trauma. We may have all we need to meet our physical needs. We may have a good job and lots of friends. We may have a nice home, drive a luxurious automobile—and yet be in deep pain.

For example, all the money in the world means nothing when a marital partner forsakes you for someone else, or when your own son or daughter faces the trauma of divorce. Furthermore, what joy is there in having a good job and a nice home when your children do not respond to your love or, worse yet, take advantage of what you've done for them? And the worst pain of all is to see children turn away from the Lord and follow the ways of the world.

Pain and suffering, then, are relative. And thus what James was saying to these first-century Christians is applicable to us all. He has issued a call to all twentieth-century Christians to be patient and longsuffering in the midst of our own pain. Some of it we have brought on ourselves; in other instances, there is no explanation. It just happened.

I have a friend who teaches in a Christian school. Unfortunately, his son began to run with the wrong crowd, got into drugs and ended up committing suicide. Can you imagine the pain this man and his wife felt? My own heart broke when I heard what happened.

But do you know what my friend did? He conducted his son's funeral. In the midst of that dark hour he stood before a host of teenagers and shared his love for his son, but most important he shared the gospel of Jesus Christ, the Son of God, and the folly of seeking happiness in drugs and alcohol. People who have faced severe persecution would probably testify that this man's patience and perseverance in pain surpassed their own.

Probably the most painful experience of all is to be blamed for something we did not cause. The very week I was writing this chapter I heard of a Christian who worked for a non-Christian employer who was guilty of a business practice that was unethical. Because this Christian worked closely with this individual, she felt it necessary to quit the job and not be party to his inappropriate behavior. In so doing, it was impossible to avoid exposing this man's action to a certain client. In retaliation, the employer has sued this Christian, accusing her of stealing, when in reality she was doing what she had been told to do. Here is a case where a Christian was falsely accused for taking a stand against wrongdoing. And because of this man's high position in the business world, his financial reserves and his power, he could possibly have won this case. To state it simply, this Christian was frightened. She felt she was in danger of losing certain credentials that could affect her ability to get another job. Even though she had channels in her society to defend herself, she has no guarantee that right would win out.

It's in situations like these that James has issued a call for us to *be patient* and *stand firm* and not to waver in our faith, even though the going is tough! It is during these times of difficulty that we have opportunity to evaluate where we are in our Christian growth and to think in terms of eternal values. Most important, it provides us with the opportunity to understand in a more meaningful way what the second coming of Christ will really mean. Fortunately, the story I've just related turned out well for this Christian. Many prayed for her situation and God protected her. Her former employer dropped the suit and did not puursue any kind of retaliation.

A couple of years ago, I faced the darkest period of my life. People I felt I had trusted totally attacked my character publicly. But at the darkest moment I turned everything over to God. I determined with God's help to blame no one and not to allow anger and bitterness to grow in my life. I determined to learn everything I could from the experience—to learn from my own mistakes.

And at that moment, the dark clouds of despair began to roll away and the light of God's grace reentered my soul. *Now* I thank God for every moment of that experience. It was difficult to thank God *then.* But James was right, "The Lord is full of compassion and mercy." His vindication has been incredible!

Note

1. John Blanchard, *Not Hearers Only,* vol. 4 (London: Word Books, 1974), p. 39.

11
PROVISIONS THROUGH PRAYER
James 5:13-15

Is any one of you in trouble? He should pray. Is anyone happy? Let him sing songs of praise. Is any one of you sick? He should call the elders of the church to pray over him and anoint him with oil in the name of the Lord. And the prayer offered in faith will make the sick person well; the Lord will raise him up. If he has sinned, he will be forgiven. (James 5:13-15)

In 1924, two climbers were part of an expedition that set out to conquer Mount Everest. As far as is known, they never reached the summit; and they never returned. Somewhere on that gigantic mountain they were overpowered by the elements and died.

After the failure of the expedition, the rest of the party returned home. Addressing a meeting in London, one of those who returned described the ill-fated adventure. He then turned to a huge photograph of Mount Everest, mounted on the wall behind him. "Everest," he cried, "we tried to conquer you once, but you overpowered us. We tried to conquer you a second time, but again you were too much for us. But, Everest, I want you to know that we are going to conquer you, for you can't grow any bigger, and *we can*!"

The spiritual application of this illustration is quite clear. Life has its periods of excitement and happiness. We also face mountains that are very difficult to climb. Sometimes they defeat us! True, these "mountains" vary in size, but in many respects they can grow no larger than God allows. On the other hand, as Christians we can grow "bigger" in our approach to these problems. This is part of the process of becoming mature in Christ.

The Christians James wrote to in the first century were facing some gigantic "mountains." All along, James has been telling them how to conquer these obstacles. And in this paragraph in chapter 5 (vv. 13-15), he elaborated on what he had already spoken on in the opening verses of his letter—God's provisions through prayer. In the context of discussing "trials of many kinds," he exhorted them to seek wisdom through prayer (see 1:2-8). In chapter 5, he became more specific. Let's take a closer look.

THREE QUESTIONS (James 5:13-15)

James discussed three questions in this paragraph: being "in trouble"; being "happy"; and being "sick." Relative to these conditions, he raised three questions and then gave three answers. Let's look first at the questions.

"Is Any One of You in Trouble?" (James 5:13a)

The *Amplified Bible* renders James 5:13a, "Is any one among you *afflicted—ill-treated, suffering evil*?" From the context we can understand more fully what James had in mind. Many of these Christians were facing severe trials.

They were working for non-Christians who wouldn't pay them their wages (Jas. 5:4). Consequently, they were unable to meet their personal needs while their employers lived in "luxury and self-indulgence" (5:5). Some of these Christians were even being falsely accused—perhaps even sentenced to death, though innocent of any wrongdoing (5:6).

With the question, "Is any one of you in trouble?" James captured a variety of troubles many Christians face at some time in life. Who has not felt the pain of rejection from those you've reached out to in love? Who, as a parent, has not suffered mental anguish because of a wayward son or daughter? Who, as a spiritual leader, has not felt the pain that accompanies the lack of response from those you reach out to who have spiritual needs? What about daily pressures—just keeping up with the demands of life—at work, at home, at school? With this question, James covers it all. There is no affliction, no problem, no difficulty that is excluded!

"Is Anyone Happy? (James 5:13b)

This question, "Is anyone happy?" focuses on the flipside of our emotions. When we face affliction we are naturally sad, distressed, and anxious. But, thank God, there are those events in life that spark feelings of joy and happiness:

- A beautiful sunrise
- A warm touch from someone you love
- A word of encouragement
- A positive response from someone you're concerned about
- A raise in salary
- A compliment
- When your favorite football team wins
- A vacation free from lingering worry.

Life is filled with those moments that are distressful and make us sad. There are also those moments that are exciting and exhilarating. The Bible recognizes both kinds of emotion. God never planned for life—even the Christian life—to be one continuous "mountaintop experience." In fact, we wouldn't enjoy the "mountaintops" if we did not experience a few "valleys." Paul recognized this dual experience when he wrote, "Rejoice with those who rejoice," and "mourn with those who mourn" (Rom. 12:15).

"Is Any One of You Sick?" (James 5:14a)

Here James is referring to a specific kind of affliction—physical illness. The Greek word translated "sick" literally means "to be without strength; to be weak in body."

When sin entered the world it affected every aspect of life—especially our physical well-being. John Blanchard summarized it well, when he wrote: "Every fiber of man's being became prone to disease in that moment and has remained so ever since, so that there is not one atom of our physical makeup that is not now subject to disease."[1] Experience, of course, verifies this reality.

THREE ANSWERS (James 5:13-15)

James not only asked three questions, he gave three answers which all focus on God's provisions through prayer.

Petition (James 5:13b)

"Is any one of you in trouble?" His answer to this question is concise and clear. "He should pray."

This has been part of God's provision throughout human history. Listen to King David: "The cords of death entangled me; the torrents of destruction overwhelmed me. The cords of the grave coiled around me; the snares of death confronted me. *In my distress I called to the Lord;* I cried to my God for help. From his temple he heard my voice; my cry came before him, into his ears" (Ps. 18:4-6).

Listen also to Paul as he wrote to the Philippians: "Do not be anxious about anything, but in everything, by prayer and petition, with thanksgiving, *present your requests to God.* And the peace of God, which transcends all understanding, will guard your hearts and your minds in Christ Jesus" (Phil. 4:6-7).

There is no problem, no concern, no affliction that is too small to warrant God's concern. Think about that for a moment! Certainly He's concerned when we face the gigantic calamities of life! But He's also concerned when we face the minor struggles. Read Paul's words again! "Do not be anxious about *anything,* but in *everything,* by prayer and petition, with thanksgiving, present your requests to God." The words *anything* and *everything* are all-inclusive in meaning. That means God is interested in *every* detail of my life—and yours!

Joseph Scriven captured this truth when he wrote:

Have we trials and temptations?
Is there trouble *anywhere*?
We should never be discouraged,
Take it to the Lord in prayer.

Can we find a friend so faithful
Who will all our sorrows share?
Jesus knows our *every* weakness,
Take it to the Lord in prayer.[2]

Praise (James 5:13c)

The answer to James's second question also focuses

on prayer—another aspect of prayer. "Is anyone happy?" he asked. "Let him sing songs of *praise.*" In essence James was saying that if we are enjoying life in a special way, we should not forget the Source of that happiness. We should praise the Lord! Again, listen to David: "Give thanks to the Lord, call on his name; make known among the nations what he has done. Sing to him, sing praise to him; tell of all His wonderful acts. Glory in his holy name; let the hearts of those who seek the Lord rejoice" (1 Chron. 16:8-10).

And again listen to Paul: "Speak to one another with psalms, hymns and spiritual songs. Sing and make music in your heart to the Lord, always giving thanks to God the Father for everything, in the name of our Lord Jesus Christ" (Eph. 5:19-20).

It should be noted at this point that "petition" and "praise" are not mutually exclusive concepts, related only to our specific needs and moods. In moments of joy, we should not forget to ask God to keep us from pride. And in moments of weakness we should not forget to praise the Lord. In fact, we can experience emotional healing when we get our minds off ourselves and focus our thoughts on God—His greatness, His love, His character!

Paul Billheimer captured this point when he wrote, "Here is one of the greatest values of praise: It decentralizes self. The worship and praise of God demands a shift of center from self to God. One cannot praise God without relinquishing occupation with self. Praise produces forgetfulness of self—and forgetfulness of self is health."[3]

Intercession (James 5:14-15)

James's third question and answer are probably the basis of more controversy and confusion than any other area of Christian theology. "Is any one of you sick [physically ill]?" he asked. Once again he answered his own question, "He should call the elders of the church to pray over him and anoint him with oil in the name of the Lord. And the prayer offered in faith will make the sick person well; the Lord will raise him up. If he has sinned, he will be forgiven" (Jas. 5:14-15).

There are at least two basic reasons why James's answer is confusing and controversial to some Christians. The first is based upon objective thinking; the second is based on subjective thinking. On the objective side of the ledger, the Bible says a lot about physical healing. In fact, a major part of Jesus' miraculous acts involved healing people physically. We also see some of God's appointed leaders—particularly the apostles—healing people of physical ailments.

On the subjective side of the ledger, physical illness is very threatening. The prospect of dying is frightening, whether it involves ourselves personally or a loved one. When facing death, we desperately want help. For most of us, there is no price too great to pay! There is no avenue we will not pursue! A dying man or woman will respond to any ray of hope. And since the Bible speaks of healing (miraculous healing), and since the Bible speaks of the power of faith (faith to heal), and since the Bible tells us God can do anything, it is only natural to want His help when facing the results of a crippling disease or disaster or when facing the prospect of death.

The desire to seek God's help in times like these *is* natural. More so, it is biblical! It is God's will. We *should* ask for prayer! We should ask for healing! James could not be clearer. A Christian who is facing serious illness should "call the elders of the church to pray over him and anoint him with oil in the name of the Lord."

THREE REALITIES

The problem we face as Christians is to understand

what James meant in this passage. To do so, there are certain realities we must face—biblically, experientially, and rationally.

A Biblical Reality

Not everyone who prayed for physical healing in New Testament times was actually healed—including some of God's choicest servants. The Apostle Paul stands out as a supreme example. God actually worked miracles through Paul in healing others. However, there came a time in his own life when he actually "pleaded with the Lord" to remove what he identified as a "thorn in the flesh." We do not know what this "thorn" actually was, but some have speculated it may have been serious disfiguration or perhaps an eye disease. Whatever, the Lord's response to Paul's prayer was not healing. Rather, it was the power and strength to cope with the problem. Thus, the Lord responded, "My grace is sufficient for you, for My power is made perfect in weakness" (2 Cor. 12:9).

No place in Scripture does God promise to always heal. Furthermore, it is not correct doctrine to teach that there is healing in atonement. There are those who believe that it is God's intention that His children always experience perfect health. They base their belief primarily on Matthew's statement, which is also a quote from Isaiah, "He took up our infirmities and carried our diseases" (Matt. 8:17).

It is true that Jesus took upon Himself all of our sins and the *results* of our sins—which certainly includes bodily deterioration. But this does not mean we are promised a physical body that will not deteriorate in this life. Rather, it means—to quote Paul, "That if the earthly tent we live in is destroyed, we have a building from God, an eternal house in heaven, not built by human hands" (2 Cor. 5:1). Christ's death and resurrection guarantees that the Christian will have a new body someday—one that will never perish or deteriorate.

Thus, to teach that it is not God's will for Christians to be physically sick is not a correct interpretation of Scripture. To arrive at this conclusion means ignoring or misinterpreting great portions of the Bible.

An Experiential Reality

Not only is it impossible to find this doctrine in the Bible—that is, that it is God's will that we should never be sick—but the *experience* of many committed Christians demonstrates that this is not true.

Recently, I was visiting with a man who shared with me that his pastor had just died from a serious disease. Interestingly, he attended a church that taught that Christians need not be sick if we have enough faith. The pastor himself taught this doctrine. In his final days, he mustered all the faith he could, and so did the church. But the pastor died. "I guess we didn't have enough faith," the man said with a note of guilt in his voice. At that moment I had the opportunity to minister to this man, to share with him from Scripture that it was not his fault, the pastor's fault, or the church's fault that the death occurred. Rather, within the providence of God, it was not the Lord's will for this man to continue to live.

There are thousands of Christians—probably millions—who seriously pray for a loved one's healing, but the person does not get well and eventually dies. The sad part is that, for some, the sense of failure and guilt is almost more than they can bear. *False doctrine* always creates *false guilt.* On the other hand, *true doctrine* frees us from both *false guilt* and *real guilt.* And may I remind you that false guilt that is related to death and dying is the most intense kind of guilt there is.

A Rational Reality

There's a third factor that must be considered in understanding what James is teaching. To teach that it is not the will of God that a Christian be sick is illogical and irrational. If this were true, we would have to conclude—to be consistent in our thinking—that it is not the will of God that a Christian should ever die. This conclusion, of course, is totally out of harmony with what the Scripture teaches and certainly is not verified by experience (1 Thess. 4:13-18).

WHAT THEN IS JAMES TEACHING?

He is teaching at least four important truths:

First, when a Christian is seriously ill, he should definitely have the freedom to call for the elders of the church to pray. Note that these men were not "professional healers" who went from place to place conducting healing meetings. In fact, nowhere in Scripture do we have examples of what we see today in many healing meetings. James was not referring to a public situation. Rather, the elders were to go to the sick person and pray. In New Testament days it probably was in the home. Today it may be in the home or in a hospital room.

However, this does not mean that we cannot nor should not pray for people publicly. But it is strange indeed that many people who claim to have the "gift of healing" do not *go* to the sick, but insist that the sick *come* to them. This practice seems to raise some very serious questions from a biblical point of view.

Second, the elders were to anoint the sick person with oil. It is easy to understand James's exhortation to pray for sick people. It is more difficult to understand what he meant when he said they were to anoint with oil.

The word that James used, which is translated "anoint," actually means to "rub." Therefore, he was probably referring to the ancient custom of rubbing the sick person with olive oil. It was a means whereby they attempted to help the sick person feel better.

We must remember that in New Testament days, they were very limited in their medical knowledge and practice. They did not have access to all of the marvelous antibiotics and other healing ingredients that are at our disposal today. All they could do was to attempt to make the sick person more comfortable. Sensitively rubbing the body brought a certain amount of relief from distress.

Today, we *do* have access to medical help unknown in the ancient world. To apply James's teaching directly, then, means helping a sick person gain access to every possible means of physical help through modern medical knowledge and assistance.

There is an indirect implication to this truth. Oil can be used symbolically in the context of prayer. At Fellowship Bible Church our elders apply this truth both directly and indirectly. We certainly encourage medical help. But we also use oil symbolically as we pray for the sick. In this sense, it is similar to the waters of baptism. The baptismal tank *represents* the grave. Oil can be used to *represent* life and healing.

Third, the elders were to pray for the sick person in "the name of the Lord." To pray in "the name of the Lord" is a very profound concept. It does not simply mean *invoking* the name of the Lord. Rather, it means praying according to the "will of God." It means recognizing that God is sovereign, "That at the *name of Jesus* every knee should bow" (Phil. 2:10). No man or woman has a right to dictate to God what He must do. We can only entreat Him and pray that He will do what is ultimately best for all of us. James, then, is instructing the elders to approach a sick person with humility, realizing that God is ultimately in control of human destiny.

Fourth, the elders were to pray "in faith." This is a concept that often confuses Christians, particularly relative to healing. They interpret "faith" as belief without any element of doubt. First, this is probably impossible for any human being. Our faith is always mixed with human weakness. Fortunately, God sees beyond our human limitations and honors what faith we have—just as Jesus did for the man who came to Him confessing, "I do believe; help me overcome my unbelief!" (Mark 9:24). Jesus honored this request and healed the man's son who had been controlled by an evil spirit.

However, if we understand God's power and the fact that He can do anything, it is not difficult for any Christian to pray for healing "in faith." However, to be able to pray with this kind of faith means understanding God's sovereignty. We must acknowledge that God responds to our faith *in His ability* to heal—not to our faith that He is *going to heal* in every situation. If we have to have enough faith to believe that God will heal in every situation, no man or woman would have sufficient faith, for we do not know for sure what God's will is in the matter. The facts are that we know from Scripture that it is *not* the will of God to heal in every situation. How then can we have faith to believe that He is *going* to do so?

On the other hand, we know from Scripture that God can do anything He wants to. He is not limited by natural law. We know that if He so chooses, He can and will heal—and as strange as it may seem, He heals in response to *our prayers*.

Over the years I have participated in prayer sessions for sick people. With the elders of our church I have anointed people with oil (symbolically speaking) and have prayed in the name of the Lord for healing. On occasions I've seen God answer our prayers in marvelous ways. On the other hand, I've seen the Lord take home to heaven the person for whom we have so diligently prayed.

On those occasions when God has not healed, we must humbly accept the will of God. We must not feel it is a lack of faith on our part or on the part of the one who is ill. We must not blame ourselves or become suspicious that it's because of some sin in our lives or in the life of the one who is dying. Rather, if our hearts have been right towards God, we must accept the illness as the will of God! And in many respects, God has answered our prayers; for to deliver a soul from pain and suffering through death is a glorious release for a terminally ill person.

God has enabled me to see wonderful Christians face death with a proper biblical perspective. One such person was Joyce Millet. Joyce certainly wanted to live. Her husband Bill and her six sons certainly wanted her to live. As elders in our church, we wanted her to live. We prayed for Joyce. We anointed her with oil. But God did not choose to heal.

To her dying day, Joyce knew that God could heal her if He so chose. However, in the light of what she knew about Scripture, she prepared for her homegoing in a marvelous way. Following her death, her sister captured her biblical perspective beautifully in a special publication. She wrote:

> An experience like Joyce's of facing disease and death is not unique in this generation of rampant cancer. What is unique and inspiring is her response and life-style through the trial of terminal illness.
>
> She made several important decisions about her short future. The first was that she would not return to the hospital. Remaining at home allowed Joyce to focus upon her living opportunities rather than upon a sickroom existence. She arose daily

(until the very last), dressed, came to meals with the family, visited with friends, wrote letters in the sunny corner of her bedroom, and prepared her belongings, her family and her friends for the time she would be gone.

There was never an attitude of death in the house. Instead, there was laughter, special talks, and hope. The hope was so evident; hope not limited to desire for recovery, but hope in God's ability to keep in the palm of His hand the one who depends upon His love. Joyce lived at home. She didn't die there. All who entered the house knew what that meant.

A second decision Joyce made about her last months was that life should continue as planned. She bravely said goodbye to Jonathan who had committed his summer to mission work in Israel, and to Brian and Greg who were studying at Biola University in California. She sent her family off to their annual Colorado family camp without her. There was to be no sense of suspending things, waiting for the worst. And in His grace, God brought everyone back home before she had to say goodbye.

Thirdly, Joyce made a decision to plan for the future, choosing rather to consider the needs of others than to languish in her own pain. That's where the Christmas decorations came in. She bought all the presents for the upcoming Christmas and added to the village collection. She also made memory albums for the boys and marked historical information on pieces of furniture and special objects. She planned the distribution of her personal belongings, saying, "It gives me great pleasure to know you'll have this which God gave to me."

These decisions—to remain at home, to continue life as planned, and to consider the needs of others, made Joyce's last months triumphant.

She finished her journey with the same dignity, joy, and faith which had characterized her all along. Her husband wrote, "Beyond convenience, comfort, friendship, even love, she insisted that the right thing, that which honored God the most, be done."

What "honored God the most" was bringing Joyce home to Himself. She joined Him quietly on the morning of September 11, 1983, leaving behind apple seeds of love and faith, hopefully sown.[4]

Notes

1. John Blanchard, *Not Hearers Only*, vol. 4 (London: Word Books, 1974), p. 47.
2. Joseph Scriven, "What a Friend We Have in Jesus."
3. Paul Billheimer, *Destined for the Throne* (Fort Washington, PA: Christian Literature Crusade, 1975), p. 118.
4. Elizabeth Ettinger Peters, "Joyce Ettinger Millet," A special publication.

12

SICKNESS AND SIN

James 5:16-20

Therefore confess your sins to each other and pray for each other so that you may be healed. The prayer of a righteous man is powerful and effective.

Elijah was a man just like us. He prayed earnestly that it would not rain, and it did not rain on the land for three and a half years. Again he prayed, and the heavens gave rain, and the earth produced its crops.

My brothers, if one of you should wander from the truth and someone should bring him back, remember this: Whoever turns a sinner from the error of his way will save him from death and cover a multitude of sins. (James 5:16-20)

One morning as I was scanning the *Dallas Morning News,* I was rather startled by a lead caption entitled, "Studying Sin." The sub-caption was even more intriguing: "Author says religion, science must fight evil." The two words that stood out most forcefully to me in these captions were "*sin*" and "*evil.*"

The "author" mentioned in this article is M. Scott Peck, a noted psychiatrist. The book under discussion was his latest with a title even more intriguing—*People of the Lie*.

Several statements by Dr. Peck quoted in the article grabbed my attention even more, so much so I immediately purchased a copy of the book in order to make a more in-depth study of what he was saying. For example, he stated:

- "There's a little bit of sin and evil in all of us and a whole lot in some of us."
- "It is only when people acknowledge evil that there is hope in eliminating it."
- "We are all sinners. We cannot *not* sin. All of us, therefore, from time to time commit evil."
- "What distinguishes 'evil people' from the 'ordinary sinners' is their utter unwillingness to acknowledge their sin and bear the pain of contrition, their uncorrectability because of their refusal to admit they need correction and by the consistency and subtlety of the evil they commit."[1]

Reading this article about Dr. Peck's viewpoint and later his book, I was quite astounded by what I learned. Here was a man who admittedly, for years, "looked at everything from the viewpoint of a scientist." However, as a result of his experience with numerous counselees over the years, he came to the conclusion that personal and group problems are caused by more than physical and even psychological reasons. They have spiritual roots as well. In fact, in his book *People of the Lie* he documents several cases which he classifies as demonic possession. He firmly believes he and several of his colleagues have personally encountered people who were indwelt by Satan himself.

What is so amazing about Dr. Peck's insights is that for

years he operated as a classical psychoanalyst, very devoted to Freudian methodology and treatment. It is no secret that the concepts of "sin" and "evil" have no place in the Freudian scheme of things. Supposedly, they made no moral judgments nor do they confront and teach. Rather, they listen, reflect, and interpret—and trust this process to bring insight and change.

Though Dr. Peck has not thrown overboard his commitment to certain aspects of psychoanalytic theory, he now approaches situations much differently. This is very graphically illustrated when he shares some reflections on a case involving a girl he calls "Charlene." The following is an excerpt from his book following a caption that reads, "If I Had It to Do Over Again."

> When I worked with Charlene I knew practically nothing about radical human evil. I did not believe in the existence of either the devil or the phenomenon of possession. I had never attended an exorcism. I had never heard of the word "deliverance." The very name of evil was absent from my professional vocabulary. I had received no training on the subject. It was not a recognized field of study for a psychiatrist or for that matter, any supposedly scientific person. I had been taught that all psychopathology could be explained in terms of known diseases or psychodynamics, and was properly labeled and encompassed in the standard *Diagnostic and Statistical Manual.* The fact that American psychiatry almost totally ignored even the basic reality of the human will had not yet struck me as ridiculous. No one had ever told me of a case like Charlene. Nothing had prepared me for her. I was like an infant.
>
> I cut my eyeteeth on Charlene. She was, with-

> out question, one of the major beginnings of this book.
>
> What I learned through Charlene and during the years since is insignificant in relation to what needs to be known about human evil. But it is enough that, had I to do it over again, I would work with Charlene very differently. And, conceivably, our work might succeed.
>
> First of all, I would make the diagnosis of evil in Charlene's case with both far greater rapidity and far greater confidence. I would not be misled by her obsessive-compulsive features into thinking that I was dealing with an ordinary neurosis, or by her autism into considering for months whether or not I had uncovered a strange variant of schizophrenia. I would not spend nine months in confusion, or over a year making useless Oedipal interpretations. When I did finally come to the conclusion that Charlene's most basic and real problem was evil, I did so without any sense of authority. I do not believe that the diagnosis of evil is one that should be made lightly. Nonetheless, all that I have learned since has confirmed my then tentative conclusions. Had I to do it over again, I believe I could put my finger on Charlene's problem in three months instead of three years, and with a firmness that might possibly be healing.[2]

I'm not totally appraised of Dr. Peck's theological position, even after reading his book. However, I cannot read what he has written without concluding that something dramatic has happened in his life over the last several years which has affected the way in which he practices his profession. He now travels extensively speaking to religious groups and professional associations nationwide about the integration of science and religion, and he frequently refers to biblical statements.

However, it is clear that this man has discovered through experience what the Bible has taught for years. There is a very significant correlation between the existence of sin and evil and various kinds of illness—both physical and psychological. And James, more than any other New Testament writer, deals with this reality.

ESTABLISHING CONTINUITY (James 5:13-15)

In our previous chapter we looked at what James said about sickness in general. When we are ill we are to feel free to call for the elders of the church so that they might pray for us and anoint us with oil in the name of the Lord. From the overall teaching of the Scripture we were able to see that this is God's most basic plan for dealing with sick people. Prayer for healing is definitely in the will of God. And "anointing with oil" seemingly refers to the fact that we should make use of every scientific discovery in the field of medicine.

A careful analysis of this text and the totality of Scripture also reveals, however, that it is not always the will of God to heal sick people. Therefore, it is always important that we always pray "in the name of the Lord," which, in essence, means to pray according to God's will. Some people die in the will of God. Their death results not because of lack of faith on their part or on the part of others, nor because of specific sins in their lives—but because of the frailty of the human body and its susceptibility to disease. It is definitely in the will of God that all people die at some point in time—unless they are among those Christians who are still alive when the Lord comes again. If so, many Christians will someday be transported to heaven without experiencing natural death. It is certainly possible that many of us alive today will participate in this great event.

James, however, added another facet to help us understand sickness and death. All illness, of course, is related to the effects of sin. When Adam and Eve disobeyed God it affected the whole universe. The principle of sin is operative in every living thing, including animal life and vegetation. But James reminded these New Testament Christians—and us—that there are *specific* sins that cause illness. Thus, after discussing "sickness" and "prayer for the sick" in a general way, he states, "*If* he has sinned, he will be forgiven" (Jas. 5:15b).

A TWO-FOLD PROCESS (James 5:16-18)

Sickness that is caused by specific sins in a Christian's life should be dealt with in two ways—through confession and prayer. "Therefore," James wrote, definitely establishing continuity between his previous statements about illness and healing, *"confess your sins to each other."* And then he wrote, "Pray for each other so that you may be healed" (Jas. 5:16).

Confession

Before looking more carefully at what James means, it must be stated that this is not the biblical basis for the "confessional." Through the years some religious groups have taught that it is necessary to confess sins to another human being before we can experience God's forgiveness. Nowhere in Scripture can this be sustained. God, and God alone, forgives sins. Furthermore, we need no human intercessor priest. There is only "one mediator between God and men, the man Christ Jesus" (1 Tim. 2:5).

I was personally reared in a religious community that taught that God forgives sin only after we make restitution to people we've sinned against and after we've confessed those sins to the spiritual leader in the church. I can personally testify that I experienced a great deal of relief from guilt when I went through that process. However, I learned later it did not take that process to experience forgiveness from God. John wrote, "If we confess our sins, *he* is faithful and just and will forgive us our sins and purify us from all unrighteousness" (1 John 1:9). It is clear from the overall context, that John is referring to confessing our sins to God in order to receive forgiveness—not to a minister or a priest or some other "father confessor."

Making Restitution. What then is James teaching? It seems he is saying at least two important things that relate to his overall thrust in this passage.

First, if possible and feasible, we *do* need to confess our sins to those we have wronged and seek their forgiveness. Restitution is not necessary to receive God's forgiveness, but it is necessary to be assured of man's forgiveness. Furthermore, it is often necessary if we are to be totally free in our own conscience.

I remember an event in my own life that seems almost ridiculous now, but one that was very real to me. When I was in the second grade I remember stealing a softball from school, and then telling my parents I had found it in some out-of-the-way place. It was a very simple procedure. When I came in from recess I had the ball in my possession; I went to the cloakroom where the athletic equipment was stored, and proceeded to put it in the large pocket of my coat rather than in the equipment box. The rest is history.

Many years later, after becoming a Christian and while in college, that event periodically came to my mind. "I ought to do something about that," I said to myself. But then I would put it out of my mind, convincing myself that it was ridiculous. At the time I stole the ball, its value probably would have been about $1.59. "Furthermore," I thought, "the principal, who was still at the school, would think I was crazy."

Many years went by, and periodically the thought continued to come to mind, "Gene, you should make that right. You stole that softball." Finally, I humbled myself, wrote a letter to the principal, explained the situation, and included four dollars.

Several months later I was in my hometown and met the principal. He approached me and, with tears in his eyes, thanked me for my letter. "What you have done," he said, "has helped make all of my efforts as principal over the years worthwhile." Unknown to me, at the time he received my letter he was going through some very severe problems professionally. God used my letter not only to set me free in my own conscience but to bring a measure of healing and encouragement into this man's life.

Don't misunderstand! If we tried to make everything right we've ever done wrong, we'd be spending the rest of our lives introspecting and responding. I'm not suggesting that this is what James was teaching. But there are situations that should be made right. We've hurt people. We've been insensitive. We've been vindictive. We've taken advantage of others financially. We've said things behind their backs. We've hurt their reputation. We've wounded them in other ways.

Thus, James is saying, "Confess your sins to each other"—the sins we have committed against one another in order to seek human forgiveness. God may have forgiven us a long time ago. But human forgiveness may be necessary for emotional healing to take place.

Seeking Spiritual Support. Second, James is saying there are times we need to confess our faults to other Christians who will understand us, accept us in spite of our weaknesses, and help free us from the trap of sin. Obviously, this should be done with a very select group of Christians, perhaps just a close friend or two. Public confession is unwise and unnecessary *unless* the sin has been committed against the whole group. Then it is very much in order. Even then it should be done wisely, under the guidance and direction of the spiritual leaders in the church. And when it is done in this way, it can bring healing not only to the individual but to the whole church.

Prayer

Confession is the first part of the process in experiencing healing. The second part is *prayer.* "Pray for each other so that you may be healed," wrote James. And then he said, "The prayer of a righteous man is powerful and effective" (Jas. 5:16b).

This statement specifies more clearly why Christians should confess their sins and faults to *mature* believers. First, the motive behind confessions should be for prayer. The second is that the prayers of Christians who are walking in God's will are the most effective. Conversely, James clearly implied that Christians who are not in the will of God themselves will not be effective in their prayers. In fact, they will have difficulty praying. Chances are that prayer is no longer a part of their lives if they are living in sin themselves.

To make this point, James used an Old Testament illustration. He referred to Elijah and the effectiveness of his prayer life, even over the laws of nature. And it is clear from our study of his life that he was a righteous man of prayer.

But James was also encouraging these New Testament Christians with the fact that Elijah was not perfect. He was "a man just like us." He often got discouraged. At times he got angry at God. At other times he was fearful and anxious. On one occasion he became so depressed he wanted to die. Yet, God used him mightily.

James is therefore saying that "righteousness" in a Christian and "human weakness" are not incompatible. They can exist side by side in any Christian. When we fail God we need not feel we can never be used by God again. We, more than any others, need to confess our sins to God, accept His forgiveness, and proceed to be available to do His work in this world. Remember that it is only because we are not perfect that we can become empathetic and compassionate towards others who fail.

A MINISTRY OF RESTORATION (James 5:19-20)

James culminates his letter with an exhortation to Christians to be concerned about their brothers and sisters in Christ who may be straying from God's will and ways. "My brothers," he wrote, "if one of you should wander from the truth and someone should bring him back, remember this: Whoever turns a sinner away from the error of his way will save him from death and cover over a multitude of sins" (Jas. 5:19-20).

This final paragraph in James's letter not only culminates the whole letter, but his teaching about healing in the previous verses. The thrust of James's Epistle from beginning to end is to encourage Christians to live a righteous and holy life. But this final paragraph relates to the fact that flagrant and willful sin can affect a Christian not only emotionally, but physically—and even result in death.

From the whole of Scripture, and from the total context of James's letter itself, it is clear that he was not referring to spiritual death. Rather, he was referring to Christians who so violate God's spiritual laws that they get sick and die.

This is a difficult and sensitive subject. There are some spiritual leaders who equate all sickness with sin—either the sin of unbelief (lack of faith) or some other specific sin that is unconfessed. This is a cruel doctrine. There are many Christians who get sick and die because of disease that is totally unrelated to a specific violation of God's will. There is no question that it is related to the principle of sin which is operative in the universe, because all emotional and bodily weakness relates to that fact. But to tell people who are ill and dying that their sickness is definitely because of a specific unconfessed sin is the ultimate in insensitivity. In fact, I'm confident that God considers that kind of act sin in itself.

But the fact remains that the Bible does teach that some Christians in the first century got sick and died because they deliberately and willfully ignored God's spiritual laws. Writing to the Corinthians, Paul stated that the reason many were weak and sick and that some had already died was that they were making a mockery of the Lord's Supper (see 1 Cor. 11:27-32). They had turned this sacred event into a drunken and gluttonous party. And they did it continually, knowing they were violating the will of God.

The Apostle John also referred to "a sin that leads to death" (1 John 5:16). And here James, no doubt, was dealing with the same phenomenon. The important purpose, however, of this exhortation is to help restore a person who is deliberately violating God's will and wandering from the truth.

It is every Christian's responsibility to warn a fellow believer who has, either consciously or unconsciously, chosen the wrong path. But let us make sure, of course, that it is indeed sin according to God's standard, not ours. Furthermore, let us remember that our own criteria for making that judgment is the Word of God itself. And above all, let us proceed with great humility following Paul's instructions to the Galatians, when he wrote, "Brothers, if someone is caught in a sin, you who are spiritual should restore him gently. But watch yourself, or you also may be tempted. Carry each other's burdens, and in this way you will fulfill the law of Christ" (Gal. 6:1-2).

A TWENTIETH-CENTURY PERSPECTIVE

Medical science helps us understand more clearly what James himself knew existed, but perhaps could not understand as clearly as we do today. Many bodily ailments are caused by psychological stress and anxiety. In fact, some physicians believe that up to 80 percent of all physical problems are psychosomatic in origin.

The word "psycho" comes from the Greek word *psucho* and is frequently translated "soul." The word "somatic" comes from the Greek word *sōma* which is translated "body." Put together, these two concepts form the English word *psychosomatic,* which refers to both the mind (soul) and the body.

Don't misunderstand! A psychosomatic illness is not just in the mind. It is a very real physical problem. However, the source of the problem is in the mind and heart of man. For example, one man went to the doctor with a bleeding ulcer. "Doc," he said, "it must be something I'm eating." After talking with the individual for a period of time, the doctor responded, "It's not what you're eating, it's what's 'eating' you." The source of that bleeding ulcer was anxiety and stress. It began in the mind and emotions and seriously affected the body of the individual.

Note: It must be made clear that there are some psychosomatic difficulties that are not caused by specific sins in our lives. They are caused by stress and pressure and circumstances beyond our control. Furthermore, they can be caused by the sinful actions of others. For example, one of the most evil things that is happening in our culture today—and has happened throughout history—is child molestation. The statistics are staggering regarding fathers who have sexually abused their young daughters. This is a sickening and tragic event. Unfortunately, it is devastating to the child. In fact, the child often blames herself for what happened, just as children sometimes blame themselves because their parents get divorced. Sexual molestation is probably the worst sort of evil because of what it does to the young person involved.

There are many sinful acts on the part of adults that create emotional pain and hurt in innocent victims. And when it happens to children, these problems often carry over into adult life, creating various kinds of psychosomatic problems.

On the other hand, sinful and evil attitudes and actions also create problems in the life of the person who has committed sin. This also creates psychosomatic problems. This happens sometimes more frequently with sins of the "spirit" than sins that are committed with the body. For example, lingering bitterness towards others can wither our souls and harm the body. The Scriptures warn us against letting the sun go down on our wrath. Jealousy is another withering emotion. It can become extremely destructive to our physical well-being.

The book of Proverbs speaks of the effects of psychosomatic difficulties. Note the following:

- "An anxious heart weighs a man down, but a kind word cheers him up" (Prov. 12:25).
- "A cheerful look brings joy to the heart, and good news gives health to the bones" (15:30).
- "Pleasant words are a honeycomb, sweet to the soul and healing to the bones" (16:24).
- "A cheerful heart is good medicine, but a crushed spirit dries up the bones" (17:22).

SOME QUESTIONS TO THINK ABOUT

- Am I deliberately walking out of the will of God in my relationship with others, resulting in guilt, jealousy, anger, bitterness, and other negative emotions?
- Have I confessed these sins to God and accepted His forgiveness?
- Have I sought forgiveness from someone I've hurt?
- Have I forgiven someone who has hurt me, even if he has not acknowledged his sin against me?
- If I am having difficulty overcoming temptations and sins, have I confided in one or two mature Christians, seeking their prayers?

A FINAL NOTE

Any Christian who is experiencing illness and has no known sin in his life may rest assured that the problem is not rooted in unconfessed sin.

Notes

1. Helen Parmley, "Studying Sin," *Dallas Morning News,* November 12, 1983.
2. M. Scott Peck, *People of the Lie* (New York: Simon and Schuster, Inc., 1983), pp. 178-179.